PSYCHOLOGICAL TESTING

John Toplis, a chartered occupational psychologist, joined the Post Office in 1984 as head of psychological services. Aptitude and other tests form part of many of the assessment centre and other selection and development procedures for over 200,000 staff employed by the Post Office businesses.

In 1991, as part of the business development programme, John worked with external consultants on the assessment of over 100 of Royal Mail's top managers, and went on to work on similar programmes in Subscription Services Limited, Post Office Counters Limited, and Parcelforce. Throughout this period he also advised on the appointment of top managers throughout the Post Office businesses.

In 1994 John became involved with the Post Office business education programme for its top managers, and led the team designing development workshops for these top managers. In 1996 he became employee development manager for Royal Mail Anglia.

Prior to joining the Post Office, John worked at the National Institute of Industrial Psychology and at Barking College of Technology; these posts involved both the development and assessment of tests and their use for counselling, selection and development in a number of commercial and other organisations. John is a media spokesperson for The British Psychological Society, and editor of the Professional News section of the *European Work and Organisation Psychologist*.

Victor Dulewicz is a chartered occupational psychologist, a Fellow of both The British Psychological Society and the Institute of Personnel and Development, and a member of the Institute of Directors. Currently he works at Henley Management College, where he is head of the Human Resource Management and Organisational Behaviour Faculty, research director of the Centre for Board Effectiveness, and director of assessment services. He recently led a major government-funded project investigating competences for boards of directors. He also lectures on personality, team roles, and management assessment and development. In the past, he has worked as an occupational psychologist for Rank Xerox and the Civil Service Selection Board, and was for nine years manager of assessment and occupational psychology for the STC Group. As a director of the management consultancy FDA he advises many large blue-chip companies on management assessment and development, specifically on competences, psychological testing and assessment centres, and has written numerous articles on these subjects.

Clive Fletcher is Professor of Occupational Psychology at Goldsmith's College, University of London. After completing his PhD studies, he worked for some years as a consultant psychologist in the UK Civil Service before taking up his first academic post. A Fellow of The British Psychological Society and a former chairman of its occupational psychology section, he has been involved in teaching and research in the field of managerial assessment and appraisal for over 25 years, and is the author of more than 100 books, articles and conference papers in this area, among which is the IPD's standard text on *Appraisal* (2nd edn, London, IPD, 1997). He is a member of a number of journal editorial boards, including that of *People Management*. He is frequently called upon to advise government departments and other public-sector bodies, and in his capacity as a director of FDA Assessment and Development Consultants he also acts as a consultant to a wide range of organisations in the private sector on psychological assessment and on performance appraisal. He is a chartered occupational psychologist.

PSYCHOLOGICAL TESTING

a manager's guide

John Toplis
Victor Dulewicz
Clive Fletcher

Third Edition

Institute of Personnel and Development

First published 1987
Reprinted in 1988 and 1989
Second edition 1991
Reprinted in 1994
Third edition 1997

Typeset by The Comp-Room, Aylesbury
Printed in Great Britain by Short Run Press, Exeter

British Library Cataloguing in Publication Data

A catalogue record for this book is available from the British Library

ISBN 0-85292-694-4

The views expressed in this book are the authors' own and may not necessarily reflect those of the IPD.

**INSTITUTE OF PERSONNEL
AND DEVELOPMENT**

IPD House, Camp Road, London SW19 4UX
Tel: 0181 971 9000   Fax: 0181 263 3333
Registered office as above. Registered Charity No. 1038333
A company limited by guarantee. Registered in England No. 2931892

Contents

BOURNEMOUTH & POOLE
COLLEGE OF F.E.

LRC

2500605946V

658.3125

LD
SOC
SCI

TOP

Foreword

The right quality of people and overall resourcing are critical success factors in all organisations. Whether to achieve competitive differentiation, greater efficiency and performance or better teamwork, getting the right fit between role, competencies required and the individual is essential. But how does one minimise the associated risk of getting it wrong?

One primary tool is the effective selection of candidates, whether from external sources or internal ones, for promotion or transfer. However, the question for the manager remains that of how organisations are to maximise their chances of selecting the best candidate. In an attempt to find a solution many managers turn to psychological testing.

Publishing and selling tests, licences and training is a growing business. An independent guide that is not overly technical is therefore essential. This book has therefore been written expressly for managers whose knowledge and experience of psychometric tools are limited. It is not intended as a textbook, but seeks to develop the manager's awareness of the responsibilities involved in the use of tests so that they may be applied in the most appropriate manner.

People asked to do tests are increasingly concerned about how the results will be used – especially in internal processes. The objective assessment of core competencies is vital to organisations, so any process that appears to do this must be considered. Experience suggests that subjective (more personal!) feedback from line management is better received than test results. Tests are appropriate where individuals feel ownership of the results rather than simply that they are being tested. Therefore the most appropriate use of tests may be where joint ownership of results is part of a development process. *Psychological Testing* provides good practical advice on how this can be done. There have also been concerns over the potential racial/ethnic and gender bias in tests. Further coverage here of this and the legal implications is very welcome.

This all leads to a general point that although the appropriate use of tests makes good logical, economic sense in terms of 'getting it right' more often, we must consider the impact of the messages sent out when an organisation chooses to test its staff. Some of this also applies to the recruitment process, when we are trying to attract as well as select people. Applying the guidance provided in these pages helps us focus on how this may be done.

All these issues mean that the further revision of this popular and practical book, adding to its coverage of a number of topics (including top managers, IT-based systems, 360-degree feedback and teambuilding), is most welcome. In revising it the authors have built on the success of the previous editions. The new third one is an essential tool in the extremely complex and challenging world of the effective resourcing of organisations.

Ron Collard
Vice-President, Organisation and Human Resource Planning
Institute of Personnel and Development

Preface to the third edition

This preface addresses four issues. First, it describes the audiences that we have in mind when writing the book. Second, it describes general changes in the world of testing since the first edition of this book was published in 1987. Third, it repeats concerns first expressed in the preface to the second edition. Finally, it describes how the new edition is structured and the differences between the third and the second editions.

Audiences

The full title of this book, *Psychological Testing – A Manager's Guide*, indicates the main audience for whom the book is written. It is about tests that are normally used in the world of work or in activities that are associated with employment, such as career choice or planning for a change of career, or even planning for retirement. The book does not aim to cover the many tests that have been designed for use in the areas of clinical or educational psychology.

There are several reasons why the book has been written mainly for managers. One is that managers normally decide testing policy in an organisation – whether tests should be used and in what circumstances – and we believe that this book can help them make these decisions. Next there are the issues of what tests to use and how to use them. Again, we believe that the book will be helpful. The tests and test publishers referenced here are representative of leading professional standards, but we have strongly resisted the selection of some tests as 'best buys'; to be effective tests have to be (a) well designed, (b) used in appropriate circumstances and (c) used by people who are thoroughly trained in their use. Asking for a recommendation about the 'best test' is analogous to asking about the 'best medicine' or the 'best car'.

We believe that the book may also be of interest to a number of other groups. For example, there are those studying to be managers, whether in the human resource or personnel specialism, or in other functions. We have also considered the needs of those who are about to take tests for the first time and who are wondering what they might do by way of preparation.

Changes in the world of testing since 1987

The first edition was published at a time when aptitude and reasoning tests were widely used in the UK as a way of selecting for practical and clerical work. Tests also featured as part of many programmes for the selection of graduates. In contrast, relatively little use was made of personality questionnaires – while versions of the 16PF had been available for some time, the first editions of the OPQ had only just been published. At this time, The British Psychological Society approved each of the relevant training courses, considering both the design of the tests and the qualifications and experience of the trainers. Many of those trained in testing were managers who wanted to be able to use tests in their own organisation without involving the psychologists who had taken part in the design or distribution of the tests.

By the time that the second edition was published in 1991 there had been a number of important changes. For a number of reasons The British Psychological Society decided that it would not continue to approve every training course, and instead worked on the development of certificates of competence in psychological testing. The Level A certificate – dealing with reasoning and aptitude tests – had just been made available. Attainment of the certificate meant being regarded as able to decide which test or tests might be used in particular circumstances.

There were a number of other changes. One was the rapid growth in the use of personality questionnaires. Although some were well designed and were made available only to those who had attended training courses supervised by chartered psychologists, others lacked the supporting data normally associated with well-researched instruments, and were said to require little or no training in their use. Second, tests became the subject of marketing and advertising, some companies employing sales staff paid on a commission basis. Third, large numbers of 'consultants' began offering advice on the uses of tests; at best their advice was based on the short training courses originally designed so that people could use tests in their own organisations without the direct involvement of a psychologist.

There have been further changes since the publication of the second edition. The British Psychological Society continues to work on the Certificates of Competence in Psychological Testing. So far as Level A is concerned, a distance-learning package has now been published, and is reviewed in Appendix 5 of this book; plans for a certificate of competency at Level B (Personality Testing) are now well advanced. The British Psychological Society has produced reviews of ability and aptitude tests (Level A) and personality assessment instruments (Level B). So far as the use of tests is concerned, they have often featured as part of the assessment of staff during major reorganisation programmes. For example, over 10,000 managers were tested when Royal Mail re-organised in 1991, the tests and other assessment methods used varying with the grade of manager.

The Certificates of Competence in Testing and the wider use of tests in reorganisation and other programmes does not mean that standards in the use or interpretation of tests have improved. Some tests continue to be sold with little or no evidence of their technical worth, and it should be remembered that tests can do harm by selecting the wrong people or by discriminating unfairly. In addition, some 'consultants' continue to offer advice on testing on the basis of little or no training, while efforts to market tests range from 'free trials' to glossy newsletters.

Concerns

When writing the Preface to the second edition, I expressed concern about five trends. My concerns remain and, I hope, will be of value to those reading this book for the first time.

First, tests are increasingly sold by sales staff rather than by psychologists. Such staff are sometimes recruited with the promise of high earnings from commission earned on sales made; they are not subject to any professional code of conduct, and may be tempted to make claims for tests that are well in excess of those claimed by the test designers. A second trend has been the appearance of tests that are either designed or endorsed by well-known psychologists or by business or other personalities; some have lacked the full range of evidence of worth that I would consider appropriate before tests are released for general use. A third trend has been the increased use of computers to administer, score and interpret the test results. It is easy to be impressed by the amount of text generated and by the speed of production. But not only do the basic questions to be asked remain the same – 'Is the test appropriate?' and 'Has appropriate training been given to those who will be using the results?' – but there are also signs that different expert systems vary in their accuracy (see Chapter 12). A fourth trend has been the continued claims of graphologists and others to have selection methods at least as good as those offered by psychologists. However, the information offered in support of these claims is usually anecdotal and falls far short of the independent predictive validation studies that can be offered as evidence of the best psychological tests. The fifth trend has been the incorrect use of statistics to try to convince people of the worth of tests. The most common of these is the use of the correlation matrix, in which the relationship between scores on a number of tests, and performance on a number of indicators, are summarised by a series of numbers. For example, if there were scores on nine tests, and assessments on nine performance criteria such as quality and quantity of work, a total of 81 correlations could be calculated. Once the correlations have been calculated, a high correlation between a test and a performance criterion may be offered as 'proof' of the worth of the test. However, two essential points must be taken into account when evaluating this 'proof'. The first is that when a large number of correlations are calculated, some relatively large correlations will occur by chance and the same effect may not be found if a second, independent study is carried out. This point, and related issues, are discussed in Appendix 6. The second point to consider is that tests are normally used long before such studies can be carried out. Attention needs to be given to how a test has been used to make selection and other decisions pending the results of the studies – and then whether use will change in line with the results.

All in all, testing is now big business, and many organisations and individuals now depend on income from test sales. One indication is that we were threatened with legal action in connection with a survey carried out for the second edition of this book; the threat was made before the results had been collected or analysed.

How this book is structured

This edition is in three main parts. Part I is new and is an overview designed to cover all the essential issues and ideas. Part II goes into each of the main issues in more depth. The 10 appendices contain further information on specific issues.

Sections that are new or which have been substantially revised include

- the overview; the aim is to give busy executives and others an appreciation both of the potential benefits and 'downsides' of testing

- ethical, legal and social issues, including recent legislation on disability (Chapter 3)

- The British Psychological Society Certificates of Competency in Psychological Testing (Chapter 4)

- testing top managers (Chapter 9)

- testing and measurement in a wider context, including other assessment tools (such as 360-degree feedback and competencies) (Chapter 11)

- current developments and keeping informed (Chapter 12)

- a review of the distance-learning materials published by The British Psychological Society (Appendix 5)

- taking tests and receiving feedback; guidance for people taking tests (Appendix 9).

We therefore hope that this new edition will be of interest both to new and old readers. We would welcome feedback and any ideas for future editions.

The views expressed by the authors are their own and not necessarily shared by the organisations that employ them or the IPD. The illustrations of good and bad practice that are given are based on their considerable experience as consultants to a wide variety of organisations, and should not be attributed to their employing organisations or other organisations with which they are currently associated.

John Toplis
August, 1997

Acknowledgements

We wish to acknowledge the help given by Dr Jeannette James. In the second edition of this book, Dr James wrote the Appendix on Utility Analysis and made a number of constructive comments about other parts of it. In this third edition, Dr James has updated the Appendix on Utility Analysis, which is now called The Cost-Benefits of Improving Selection (Appendix 9). In addition, Dr James has written a new Appendix (6) 'Review of The British Psychological Society Level 'A' Open Learning Programme', and has been of considerable help in commenting on drafts of some of the other sections in this new edition.

Throughout this book there are frequent references to the British Psychological Society. The Society's address is:

St Andrews House
48 Princess Road East
Leicester
LE1 7DR
Tel.: 0116 254 9568

Part One: An overview

This book is about the kinds of tests that are widely used in the world of work. The tests are often used as part of a selection procedure, but they may also be used for other purposes, such as career counselling, staff development and for team building. The tests may be adminstered and interpreted by an organisation's own staff, but may be used by consultants and other advisers.

This book has been written for four main reasons. The first is to alert managers and other readers to the real benefits that can arise from 'good' testing. The second is to warn of the disadvantages and even dangers that can arise from 'bad' testing. The third is to give insight and understanding as to why testing might be 'good' or 'bad'. The fourth is to help readers decide whether they want to make use of tests in the future.

Different kinds of tests

The tests described in this book are of two types.

Psychometric tests are tests that aim to measure different kinds of mental abilities. This group of tests includes reasoning and problem-solving tests. They are characterised by having answers that can be scored as 'correct' or as 'incorrect'. The scoring process often involves totalling the number of correct answers, and comparing the total with those of groups of other people.

By contrast, psychometric questionnaires aim to measure the attitudes and preferences of an individual. This group of tests includes personality questionnaires. Answers are often made by agreeing or disagreeing with a statement such as 'I feel nervous before making a presentation to top managers'. Answers can thus reflect preferences or even behaviour. The scoring process often involves combining the replies from similar questions into scales reflecting an individual's confidence, nervousness etc. A profile of scores, often referred to as a 'personality profile', may be produced.

1

The benefits of testing

Over the years it has been shown that psychometric tests and question-naires can identify sales staff with the highest sales figures, production staff with the highest output figures, supervisors with the highest staff morale, etc. This makes the idea of testing attractive to employers and employees alike. For employers it is an important way of competing effectively – if they can attract the high performing employees while leaving the others for their competitors, this may give them an important competitive edge. For employees, there can be real benefits in having strengths identified and developed; if individuals are placed in work which makes best use of their skills and abilities, and which matches their personality, interests and values, this can dramatically affect their output, their satisfaction, their earnings and their quality of life.

Case-study 1

Some years ago one of us was asked to advise a company on how to improve its selection of supervisors. Having collected background information it became clear that the problem was a very real one. Over the years the company's manufacturing process had become more com-plicated, demanding higher levels of diagnostic skill, staff management, record keeping and reporting. By contrast, selection procedures for supervisors had deteriorated; no longer were they carefully selected, trained and monitored when they supervised for the first time; instead, those willing to help the existing supervisors had then themselves been put in charge. Several of these supervisors volunteered the information that they could not cope.

A new selection system involving a combination of psychological tests, group discussions and individual interviews brought dramatic results. Existing employees working elsewhere in the organisation were identified as having the potential to develop. As a group they excelled during training, impressing both the company training staff and external examiners. As individuals they were pleased to show what they could do, while the company was pleased to have these key vacancies filled by people of suitable calibre.

Case-study 2

An applicant for a post of management consultant was asked to com-plete a personality questionnaire as part of the selection procedure. At interview he was well dressed and appeared extremely confident and self-assured. He talked about his business success, his family and his wide circle of friends. He was the leading figure in a local charitable organisation. From the point of view of the interviewer the impression that he was making was difficult to reconcile with the picture that had been given by the personality questionnaire; this suggested an individual of extreme sensitivity. Towards the end of the interview, the personality profile was discussed with the applicant who readily agreed with the picture given by the questionnaire. He explained that, on a number of occasions, top managers had tried to persuade him to move into general management posts, but that he had not wished to be exposed to situations that would require a robust personality. The applicant's self-awareness and insight was seen as a particular strength.

Case-study 3

After leaving college, a man in his early 20s started work in a property agency. In the first year he worked hard and was given a good annual appraisal. In his second year he worked even harder but his annual appraisal indicated that he had had only an average year. In the third year he redoubled his efforts, only to be told at the end of the year that he should be considering his future. Bewildered, he sought advice from his father, who in turn asked for advice from one of us.

At interview, the son explained that he was the first to arrive in the office and the last to leave. His files were always neat and tidy and he always returned telephone calls promptly. In contrast, his colleagues arrived late, had long lunches, and worked from disorganised desks covered with papers.

A personality questionnaire confirmed the picture emerging from the interview. The son was someone who did not have original ideas, who paid attention to detail, and who was very respectful of others. In contrast the property agency wanted people with originality who could elbow their way into profitable business deals – only essential details really mattered.

The son is now working happily and successfully for a different employer with conservative values and more traditional ways of doing business.

Case-study 4

This case-study concerns the choice of tests for clerical work. A number of possible tests were available from leading test suppliers, and the decision had to be made on which test battery to use, and which test or tests within each battery. Having decided on the modern occupational skills battery, further work showed that the best value for money would be obtained by using just three of the nine tests in the battery. The case-study is reported in more detail in Appendix 1.

Some disadvantages and dangers

There is a large number of reasons why testing may be ineffective, unfair or both. Reasons include the following – often combinations of reasons may present.

- The test does not meet recognised design standards.

- The test is not appropriate; for example, the content might be inappropriate, or the test might be too difficult.

- The test may be unfair to some applicants (because of their sex, race, or disability).

- The test may be administered incorrectly (for example, allowing too much or too little time).

- The test may be scored incorrectly (examples would be to use the wrong scoring keys, to add scores incorrectly, or to compare an individual applicant's scores with the wrong norm group (eg comparing a graduate applicant with a group of top managers rather than other graduate entrants). The test result may be interpreted incorrectly – for example, it is sometimes assumed (incorrectly) that a person who likes working with numbers will be quick and accurate at figure work, and that a person who does not like working with numbers will be slow or inaccurate.

To be successful, all the above stages in a selection process have to be satisfactory. The following case-studies illustrate problems with particular stages.

Case-study 5
A major computer company felt that it should be able to supply customers with an aptitude test so that the customers could recruit good quality programming and other staff. A test was purchased from consultants by one of its overseas subsidiaries and circulated to head office staff in London. At this stage one of us saw the test and recognised the test items – they had been copied from different pages of a well-known

4

textbook on psychological testing, where they had been used to illustrate the different kinds of psychological tests that are available.

Case-study 6
Some years ago, one of us was asked to review the effectiveness of a test of dexterity which was being used to select operatives on an assembly line. The test involved screw threads, washers and nuts and the task appeared similar to the work being done on the line itself. Those who completed the selection task in the fastest times were selected. However, analysis of the test scores showed that the job performance of those with the highest test scores was actually poorer that the job performance of those with lower test scores. It was rumoured that some of the more enterprising employees had copied the test, and that relatives and friends were practising the test at a nearby house before presenting themselves for selection.

Case-study 7
In order to attract trainees, a private computer programming school offered potential students the opportunity to take an aptitude test to check whether they had the ability to succeed in a course. A large number passed, enrolled and paid their fees, but many found it difficult to find employment at the end of the course. It emerged that the test was originally designed for data-preparation staff and that the standards required to pass the test were less demanding than those required to do programming work.

Case-study 8
As part of a major reorganisation, tests were used as part of an assessment procedure for over 300 existing managers to help decide on their allocation to positions in the new organisation. It was widely known that some staff would be surplus and voluntary redundancy would be a possibility. The size of the assessment programme and the speed with which the exercise needed to be carried out meant that a number of independent consultants were recruited on a contract basis to give feedback about performance on the psychological tests that had been used, and to write a report on each manager based on discussion of the manager's performance during the assessment procedure as a whole; these reports were to be fed back to the managers, both to explain the reasons for the decisions made and to help them to plan their future.

Although all the consultants had attended the short training courses run by suppliers of psychological tests, major problems were found in their written reports dealing with the tests as well as the parts dealing with the rest of the procedure. A special team of chartered psychologists had to be recruited to rewrite the reports before they could be circulated.

By this stage we hope that readers will realise that while the concept of testing is relatively easy to grasp, the subject is potentially complex. For example, a choice of several thousand tests is now available, although in practice a few tests are widely used and others remain merely catalogue items. If you are a manager you have only a few choices.

- Ignore the subject; you may take the view that selecting the best staff doesn't matter, or you may take the view that you will simply dismiss those recruits who do not meet your standards.

- Leave the matter to someone else in your organisation; for example, testing and other forms of assessment now form part of the studies of members of the Institute of Personnel and Development (IPD), and some IPD qualified staff go on to be trained in the use of one or more tests. Training in testing can be expensive, and it does not make sense for every manager in an organisation to be trained in it.

- Get trained in testing; we would strongly recommend that you attend training that qualifies you for the certificates of competence in psychological testing issued by The British Psychological Society. Training of this kind will help you to evaluate the many possible tests available, to decide which may be of value in your organisation, to ensure that they are used and interpreted correctly, and to show you how to check on the value and fairness of the tests.

- Seek advice from consultants; we would strongly advise you to seek advice from chartered occupational psychologists with certificates of competence in psychological testing.

To complete this overview, here are some questions that are frequently asked about tests (and some answers).

Q   Are psychological tests available for every job?

A   No. There are too many different jobs for that to be possible. However, some tests cover groups of related jobs such as those involving different types of sales work. Others cover skills that occur in many jobs, such as clerical checking or interpreting graphs and tables correctly. If no 'off-the-shelf' tests are available, tailor-made tests can be designed if the numbers of applicants and vacancies warrant the costs that will be incurred.

Q So why not use tests in every selection procedure?

A For a number of reasons, several of which may apply in a particular situation. Some of the more common objections to testing are as follows:

- the cost (not just the cost of the test materials, but of attending training courses in testing and the absence from other work). However, the benefits of testing can be considerably greater than the costs.

- the effect on candidates. It is sometimes said (i) that candidates will object to being tested, particularly if they have professional or other qualifications, or (ii) that candidates will object to taking part in a procedure that becomes long and demanding because of the inclusion of tests. However, such objections are less often raised by good candidates, who are normally keen to show what they can do.

- resistance from existing employees. Some existing employees may take the view that selection from existing staff should be based on seniority alone; there can also be pressures to recruit relations and friends of existing managers and employees. Both kinds of pressure must be resisted if organisations are to be competitive and efficient.

- because tests may discriminate unfairly. However, any part of a selection procedure may discriminate unfairly, and it cannot be assumed either that tests will discriminate unfairly or that they will be the part of the selection process most likely to discriminate. Further, because test administration and scoring are standardised and objective (see Chapter 2), tests may be more consistent in their fairness than are relatively subjective methods, such as the interview.

Q What kind of pay-off can I expect from tests?

A Pay-off needs to take account of both benefits (eg reducing the turnover of staff and/or recruiting new staff whose productivity is higher) and costs (see Chapter 10). Different kinds of tests predict different aspects of future performance. For example:

- Aptitude tests involve a series of similar items, such as checking figures or understanding paragraphs of information; such tests can be a useful guide to what people are able to do and what skills they might develop.

- Trainability tests involve giving candidates a short period of intensive training after which their performance is assessed and any errors of technique noted; as the name implies, the tests can be a useful guide to training-course performance in particular.

- Personality questionnaires focus on aspects of the personality of candidates, for example the way in which they tend to relate to other people and how they feel about themselves.

- Questionnaires about attitudes and values explore yet other aspects of candidates.

Q I am interested in better selection, but it all sounds rather complicated. What is the best way forward?

A Read this book to get some background information. Then reflect on any current problems that you may have in recruiting and selecting staff. For example, have you a group of staff whose performance has been poor and/or whose turnover is high, and could better selection help to remedy this? If you think it might, why not contact an occupational psychologist for a professional opinion? (See Appendix 2.)

Q I am suspicious of experts, particularly psychologists! Can't we just buy some tests and get on with it?

A If you ask around long enough you might be able to get hold of what appear to be tests and 'get on with it'. But bear in mind that tests cannot be judged by appearance alone. For example, a questionnaire recently sold to managers to help them assess personality was put to scientific investigation and found to be of no value. Why not do the job properly and seek appropriate information from The British Psychological Society and the Institute of Personnel and Development (see also Appendices 2 and 4)?

Q But surely the chances of being misled are small?

A   There is a great deal of money to be made from selection methods, and none of the consultants or others selling techniques for assessing staff will lack confidence in their products. Among the methods used to impress potential clients are the following:

- charging very large fees (anything costing that much must be the ultimate selection method!)

- charging low fees and relying on a high volume of sales (you don't need psychologists and expensive training courses – here is something that is practical and self-explanatory!)

- the production of testimonials (any selection method will get it right sometimes – so do the testimonials come from people who are expert in the evaluation of selection methods?)

- the production of lists of references to publications and articles (remember that some scientific and professional journals have an editorial advisory panel of experts to help to check the worth of claims made; in contrast, other journals and magazines may not seek such technical advice and may be interested only in articles likely to increase their circulation)

- the production of books that endorse the technique or approach (again, sales may have been the main editorial consideration)

- the idea that the technique can reveal 'the truth' about the candidate, getting behind what the candidate would wish to be known and perhaps revealing information unknown even to the candidate; the origins of 'the truth' may be the time and date of birth of the candidate, appearance, body movements and gestures, handwriting and so on; often the need for training in the techniques is emphasised

- the need for training is often emphasised for other techniques, including those that may originate from, or be associated with, clinical psychology; again, the appeal of such techniques is the belief that they will help to reveal 'the truth'

- the offer of a free trial of the methods, usually involving the person who will decide whether or not the technique will be used; the consultants are obtaining a degree of commitment by the trial itself; whatever the picture given few are likely to argue with it (see Chapter 4)

- the production of spurious scientific evidence; many managers do not understand the key terms 'reliability' and 'validity' which are used in the assessment of selection procedures, and this lack of knowledge can be exploited. For example, managers may relax simply because these key words have been used, and not check that they have been used properly. The effect may be compounded if statistics are added – fewer still can judge whether the statistics are appropriate

- presenting the methods well; it seems to add to the credibility of the procedure if, for example, the assessment involves the use of a small business computer and the results can be presented on a computer printout and/or in the form of a profile.

Since many reputable psychological tests have at least some of the above characteristics it is virtually impossible for the untrained manager to distinguish between selection methods that are valid and those which are not (see Chapter 1). Many well-known industrial and other organisations are currently using unproven methods.

Part Two: The main issues

1
What are tests?
(i) Characteristics and technical features

This chapter gives a brief history of psychological tests and goes on to outline the characteristics and technical features of psychological tests and questionnaires. It comprises the following sections:

- brief history

- what is a psychological test?

- properties of psychological tests

- availability of psychological tests.

Brief history

Psychological tests are not, as some people believe, a new and questionable device imported from the USA. It is just over 100 years since Sir Francis Galton, a cousin of Charles Darwin, published *Inquiries into Human Faculty and its Development*, and almost exactly 100 years since Munsterberg used tests to select tram drivers in Austria. Some 80 years ago Binet, a Frenchman, constructed the first intelligence test, a forerunner of today's ability tests.

Personality questionnaires have been around almost as long. The first such instrument used as a selection tool was Woodworth's Personal Data Sheet, a rough screening device for identifying seriously neurotic men who would be unfit for the American Army during the First World War. Indeed, the two world wars provided a major impetus in testing, recruiters on both sides of the Atlantic being faced with a massive need for assessments, and very little time. Tests and questionnaires were used to allocate men to posts most appropriate to their abilities, and as part of the procedure to select officers.

Following the Second World War, there was steady growth in the use of tests in the USA in both the public sector and by private organisations. However, in the early 1960s, the growth was checked because of stringent equal opportunities legislation, and fear of court action while the legal situation was clarified. Subsequently there appears to have been a resurgence of interest and application. For example, a survey from the American Society for Personnel Administration, reported in *Personnel Management* in April 1987, shows that a growing number of US companies are using tests. The largest increase has been in the area of personality and psychological testing; in 1986, 32 per cent of companies surveyed used such tests, compared with 22 per cent in 1985. Recent research into the costs and benefits of selection has shown that major benefits can result from testing.

In the United Kingdom, the main test users have been the Forces, the Civil Service and some large public corporations, although significant numbers of private organisations have also used tests quite extensively. In both the UK and the USA a considerable increase in test usage by the private sector has been apparent over the last ten years. For a recent picture of management selection methods in top British and French companies, see Shackleton and Newell (1991).

There are now more than 5,000 psychological instruments produced in the English language, but the vast majority of these are available for use by qualified psychologists only.

What is a psychological test?

The British Psychological Society (BPS) has a key role in controlling the publication of professionally produced test materials. In 1983 the BPS Bulletin contained the following definition of a test:

> The term psychological test refers to a procedure for the evaluation of psychological functions. Psychological tests involve those being tested in solving problems, performing skilled tasks or making judgements. Psychological test procedures are characterized by standard methods of administration and scoring. Results are usually quantified by means of normative or other scaling procedures[1] but they may also be interpreted qualitatively by reference to psychological theory.
>
> Included in the term psychological test are tests of varieties of: intelligence; ability; aptitude; language development and function; perception; personality; temperament and disposition; and interests, habits, values and preferences.

---

1 These terms are explained later in this chapter.

The BPS definition thus embraces a wide range of tests and questionnaires under the overall heading of psychological tests. This book will concentrate on those instruments that are available to non-psychologists and for which training is available; however, other instruments that are of value in occupational assessment but which can be used only by accredited psychologists will be mentioned from time to time.

Properties of psychological tests

This section deals with the fundamentals of psychological tests which distinguish them from the plethora of other paper-and-pencil instruments used in personnel and training departments. For a more detailed treatment of the nature and construction of psychological tests, see Anastasi (1982) or Kline (1986).

At this point it would be useful to differentiate 'psychological tests' between psychometric tests and psychometric questionnaires. Cronbach (1984) has proposed a useful distinction between tests of maximum performance, eg mental ability tests, and tests of habitual performance, eg personality questionnaires. Tests of maximum performance usually measure intelligence or special abilities, and have correct answers so that, broadly speaking, the higher the score the better the performance; as a group, such tests will be called 'psychometric tests' during the remainder of this book when specific reference is necessary.

In contrast, tests of habitual performance (questionnaires) tend to be designed to measure personality characteristics, interests, values or behaviour, and therefore an ability is not being stretched to get a high score. With questionnaires a high or a low 'score' signifies the extent to which a person possesses qualities such as co-operation or determination, and the appropriateness of the replies will depend on the vacancy to be filled. Some questionnaires measure bi-polar scales, such as Introversion–Extraversion; replies indicate an individual's position on each scale. As a group, such tests will be called 'psychometric questionnaires' during the remainder of this book when specific reference is necessary.

Psychometric tests and questionnaires share the same essential properties. First, they tend (with a few exceptions that are beyond the scope of this book) to be objective, standardised measures – they require a highly controlled, uniform procedure for administration and scoring. For every candidate, the test items and instructions should be the same; the time allowed should be the same if it is a timed test; the physical test conditions should be the same, ie adequate lighting, a comfortable temperature, no distractions whatsoever, plenty of work space; and so on.

A second feature of proper ability and other psychometric tests is that the test items will be ordered in level of difficulty so that candidates can get settled into the test more easily, and weaker candidates are not faced with overly complex items early on; they have an opportunity to demonstrate what they are able to do. The difficulty level is determined objectively during the pilot (design) stage of construction by calculating the percentage of those taking the test who got an item correct. In the final versions of the tests, items are re-ordered according to these percentages so that, for example, an item that 95 per cent of the pilot sample got correct would be placed very early on, whereas an item which was answered correctly by only 5 per cent of the sample would come very close to the end; thus, when there are time limits, only people with a very high ability at this type of problem-solving are faced with such a difficult item.

Third, psychometric tests and questionnaires are usually scored objectively. The administrator has a key which contains the right answers for the test, or the value to be given to a specific answer on a multiple-choice questionnaire. Thus, with objectively scored instruments, the scorer's judgement does not lead to variations in score, and indeed many instruments these days can also be machine-scored (see Chapter 12).

A fourth major determinant of objectivity and standardisation is the way in which a score is interpreted. The number of items correct on an ability test, or the sum of values for responses on a questionnaire scale, constitute a raw score which has significance only when it is compared to the range of scores obtained from a large representative sample of people for whom the test was designed. The sample might be drawn from the general population or from more specific groups – such as UK graduates or craft apprentices – and is known as the standardisation sample. The results constitute norms which, as the name implies, relate all scores to the normal or average performance of the group, and the degrees of deviation above and below the average. It is important that precise information is given about the way that the norms were drawn up – for example, norms for 'supervisors' could be based on those working as supervisors, those appointed as supervisors, those called to a selection procedure for supervisors, or all applicants for supervisory work.

A normative score is read from a norms table and is not open to the subjective interpretation of the tester. The most widely used normative scale is the percentile score, which is a rank order scale reflecting the proportion of the reference group who obtained a lower score than the individual being tested. So if a graduate applicant scored at the 65th percentile on a particular test, using UK graduate norms, his score would be better than 65 per cent of UK graduates.

A fifth characteristic of psychometric instruments is that they should have manuals that contain scientific, objective data to demonstrate how good the test is, and to what extent it does what it is supposed to do. Two critical concepts are the test's reliability and validity. Reliability refers to stability and consistency of results obtained and it can be assessed in several diffferent ways. In the 'test-retest' method of assessing reliability a large group of people is tested and then retested, using the same test, several weeks later. The initial experience of doing the test is likely to improve the group performance on the second occasion; however, if the relative positions of individual scores are found to be very different on the two occasions, the reliability of the test would be suspect.

A good test manual will contain empirical evidence of the test-retest reliability, showing the degree of similarity between the results obtained from the first and second administration of the tests to the same sample, and also the degree of internal consistency, using the split half method. This involves comparing the scores obtained on one half of the items (normally the odd-numbered items) to the scores obtained on the other half (the even-numbered items). This figure will reflect the internal consistency of the test, ie whether or not its items all measure the same broad characteristic.

During the design stage of a reputable psychometric instrument great care is taken to ensure that only the items that are measuring the same broad ability are retained for a specific scale. As part of this process, attention needs to be paid to the way in which the questions are presented; for example, if some of a trial group were to get all the items of a similar format wrong it would be a sign that these items might be measuring a separate ability, and this possibility would need to be checked.

The sixth characteristic of a psychometric instrument is that its validity has been assessed objectively. Validity is undoubtedly the most important question when choosing a test for occupational assessment and it is a measure of how far the test measures what it was designed to measure. In the occupational context, validity is usually demonstrated by relating the score on a test given prior to employment to some sort of external measure of work performance, eg appraisal ratings of job performance, quasi-objective measures such as sales figures or ratings of performance on a training course, where successful completion of the course is a prerequisite for job success.

If the performance measure is obtained some time after the test has been taken, the validity measure that can be calculated is the predictive validity. This is the extent to which a test can predict future behaviour because it takes account of the wide range of factors that a job incumbent is exposed to, and is influenced by. Predictive validity is regarded as the best single measure of the worth of a test.

There are often a number of practical reasons, especially time pressure, why it is not possible to do a predictive validation study, and so a concurrent study (in which the test and performance measures are taken at the same time by existing staff) has to suffice. While concurrent validity gives a fairly good indication of the relevance of a test to work performance, it is not as good a measure as a predictive validity because the test performance of existing staff may be affected by skills and other behaviours acquired during the current employment rather than aptitude or trainability.

When selecting a psychometric test or questionnaire for a specific purpose the most important data in the manual are those relating to validity. Look to see if the instrument shows good validity data on a group of employees similar to the one that you wish to assess; try not to rely on job titles alone as these can be misleading – for example, in the Post Office, executive grade staff are middle managers rather than top managers. Ideally the number involved in the validation study should be at least 100 and the correlation between test scores and the criteria of performance should be at least 0.2 (see Chapter 6). If the correlation is lower, it is unlikely that the use of the test will be financially worthwhile (see Chapter 10 and Appendix 8).

One final issue on validity is that of face validity, which refers to the extent to which the instrument looks as if it is measuring something relevant to the job. Unfortunately, psychometric tests and questionnaires are sometimes judged only on their appearances and as the graphic design of some unproven 'tests' is at least as good as the best of the proven tests, errors of judgement can be made. Face validity is nevertheless of some importance – if an instrument has a low face validity or contains items which might, for example, appear bizarre or intrusive to respondents, then its acceptability to candidates will be questionable and this might well affect their motivation and hence undermine the validity of the results. For example, the use of an 'inkblots' test on graduates or managers often arouses reactions of mirth, irritation or even hostility, and can affect their attitude not only to the specific test but to the entire test procedure.

Information on face validity does not usually appear in psychometric test and questionnaire manuals. In this matter, users have to exercise their own judgement about the potential suitability of an instrument to a particular group of employees. One way around this problem (and another problem when it is not possible to validate an instrument) is to look for an instrument that measures the same characteristic (as denoted by a statistically significant correlation) as another which has already been shown to be valid on a similar group. Most manuals contain the correlations between the test or questionnaire and other similar instruments. If the new instrument is more acceptable, and correlates highly with the unacceptable one, then this can be used in its place with some confidence. Nevertheless, a specific validation study should still be set up wherever possible.

In summary, a 'true' psychometric test or questionnaire can be distinguished in the following ways:

● It is supplied by a reputable publisher only to those who have received training in its use.

● It is supplied with instructions for administration, scoring and interpretation (including norms).

● It is supplied with details of its reliability and validity.

In addition, the 'face validity' of an instrument can be important in determining its acceptability both to the candidates and others who have to endorse the selection process and make use of information arising from it.

Under normal circumstances, managers should use only 'true' tests. When this is not possible or practicable, they should retain an occupational psychologist to identify, trial and evaluate possible new tests (see Appendix 2).

Availability of psychological tests

'True' tests are carefully designed and developed and, unless they are used by fully qualified or adequately trained staff, their value will be strictly limited and their security jeopardised. The British Psychological Society, with the assistance and full support of the reputable test suppliers, has sought to maintain standards.

To be eligible to obtain test materials one is required to attend special courses. Training in the use of tests of maximum performance (Level A tests of ability or aptitude) normally takes about a week, and constitutes an entry requirement for further courses in the use of tests of habitual or typical performance (Level B personality and interest questionnaires). A generic course in the latter also lasts about one week, although some providers offer courses in a modular format. Courses are designed and run by chartered occupational psychologists, who are individually responsible for their standard and scope to The BPS. Attendance on these courses is a major stepping stone towards the attainment of a certificate of competence for Level A and Level B tests, awarded by The BPS. Further details of courses and BPS certificates appear in Chapter 4.

One final cautionary point – attendance at any Level A or Level B course is a necessary, but not sufficient condition for ordering and using any test at a given level. Test publishers usually require some additional training for their tests if the tester has not attended one of their training courses.

Summary

Psychological tests are well established and a wide choice is available. There is consensus about the technical properties and characteristics to be checked when choosing a particular test. The British Psychological Society exercises rigorous control over the training required for the certificate of competence in occupational testing for Level A tests (aptitude tests) and for Level B tests (personality and interest questionnaires).

2
What are tests?
(II) Types of test and outline descriptions

This chapter begins with a classification of available psychometric tests. The types of tests are then discussed and outline descriptions given of some of the better-known tests in each category. It must be stressed that these illustrative descriptions are not an endorsement of the tests and that their technical qualities and relevance to particular circumstances must be carefully assessed. Furthermore, it is not a comprehensive list of all the tests available in the UK.

The second part of the chapter deals with psychometric questionnaires in a similar way.

Those who wish to have background information about the research into mental abilities from which these tests have been derived should read Appendix 3.

Psychometric tests are divided into:

(i)   Tests of attainment

(ii)   Tests of general intelligence

(iii)   Tests of special ability or aptitude
        – tests of aptitude for special kinds of work/job
        – test batteries.

Psychometric questionnaires can take the form of:

(iv)   Personality questionnaires

(v)   Interest questionnaires

(vi)   Values questionnaires.

In addition, other approaches to personality assessment are described in outline, with references for further reading.

Psychometric tests

From the section above, it will be clear that there are various broad types of tests of mental ability (maximum performance) available: General Intelligence tests; tests of special aptitude or ability; tests of aptitude for specific jobs; and tests of attainment or proficiency.

Tests of attainment

Tests of attainment, which incidentally are not included in the BPS definition of a test (above) but have similar properties and are widely used, are designed to measure the degree of knowledge and/or skill a person has acquired at a particular point in time. School examinations are one type of such a test. They are very much concerned with experience and learning, and the level of proficiency acquired at certain tasks or skills. Tests of intelligence or aptitude, on the other hand, are designed in theory to provide a measure of an individual's capacity to learn (knowledge and skills) or to perform a skilled task in the future, irrespective of present training and experience. In practice, however, because such tests are based upon tasks incorporating verbal, numerical or symbolic information they rarely, if ever, provide measures that are completely uninfluenced by previous experience and education. It is perhaps helpful to envisage a continuum, with pure attainment tests on one side, say on the left, and pure psychological tests of aptitude on the other, on the right. Thus, a test of mathematical attainment involving knowledge of basic mathematical principles would lie to the left of centre and an O-level maths exam might lie a little further to the left, but neither would be at the end, because the person's numerical reasoning ability would also affect performance on these attainment tests. Similarly, a numerical reasoning test would lie to the right of the continuum, but not quite at the extreme because knowledge and experience of working with figures at school would probably have some effect on performance.

Psychometric tests are therefore designed to assess capacity rather than existing knowledge and skill. To give an understanding of the different types of tests of intelligence, special aptitudes or abilities and tests of aptitudes for specific jobs, examples will be described in sections below. Examples will also be given of the more widely used tests which have proved to be valuable for assessment and counselling purposes. Some tests are designed for use with the general population, to discriminate across the entire ability range, whilst others are designed to discriminate most effectively within specific sections of the range, for example among graduate or management populations; in tests designed for the latter groups the types of mental operations called for are of a much higher order of complexity, such as reasoning and evaluation (Guilford in Appendix 3).

When considering tests it is important to look at the tests and the test manuals and not make decisions only on the basis of the test title. In particular, most tests have instructions which demand a knowledge of language, and it is, for example, difficult to design numerical items free of verbal skills.

Tests can either be used alone or in combination with other tests according to the quality or qualities to be measured. Combinations of tests are called test batteries. Some test batteries comprise tests that have been designed for use together and which may have similar instructions, answer sheets, etc. Often a single manual gives details about all the tests in the battery and gives information about combinations of the tests to be used for common vacancies, such as those for apprentices or graduate entrants. Following a review of the different broad types of test, test batteries are considered further.

Tests of general intelligence

There is a multitude of different definitions of intelligence, but the simplest and most appropriate for practical purposes is 'the capacity for abstract thinking and reasoning with a range of different contents and media'. The specific scientific identification and measurement of intelligence is nowadays carried out using a statistical technique called factor analysis, to determine the general intelligence component across a number of different tests. Further information about mental abilities is given in Appendix 3.

It usually takes between 30 and 60 minutes to obtain a reliable measure of general intelligence. Most intelligence (and aptitude) tests are administered to groups, require written responses and are timed. Items are usually presented in verbal, numerical and symbolic/diagrammatic form, thus sampling a range of different formats. The written response normally involves marking one of a number of possible correct answers but a few tests require candidates to write the correct answer (these are known as open-ended).

Examples of the more popular types of item format in tests of general intelligence are given below.

Verbal
(a)   Analogies
        Child is to parent as kitten is to . . .

(a) Bitch (b) Mouse (c) Cat (d) Terrier (choose one)

(b) Synonyms
   Which of the following means the same as 'tired'
   (a) Fatigued (b) Hot (c) Energetic (d) Stiff (choose one)

Non-verbal:
(a) Number Series
   Fill in the missing number in the series below:
   2 4 7 11 ... 22

(b) Diagrammatic/Symbolic Reasoning
   Which of the following should be added to complete the series of
   diagrams below: 1, 2 or 3?

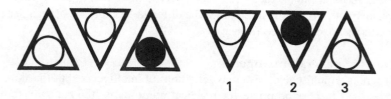

Some psychometric tests contain all these types of items, and others as
well, whilst some so-called 'culture fair' tests contain only symbolic or
diagrammatic items in an attempt to overcome the problems associated
with candidates from different, non-Western cultures and/or those
whose first language is not English. This is a major issue in testing and
is discussed in Chapter 3.

There is a wide variety of tests of general intelligence available, and
the choice of which one to use depends largely on the educational level
of applicants, their previous experience and the jobs for which they are
being considered.

Examples of two such tests, designed to discriminate across the general
population are:

• AH4: Verbal, Numerical and Diagrammatic Items (Source: 2)*

• Raven's Standard Progressive Matrices: A non-verbal test, with diagrammatic items, in matrix form (4, 6).

* Details of the test publishers referenced in the text appear in Appendix 4.

These two tests are designed for individuals with average ability and are suitable for general personnel selection. However, if one needs to assess the general intelligence of clearly above-average individuals such as graduates, managers and research staff the following tests are more suitable:

- AH5/AH6: Verbal, numerical and diagrammatic items. AH6 has two equivalent forms, one for scientists, engineers and mathematicians, the other for those with an arts background (Source: 2)

- Compound Series Test: A non-verbal test with diagrammatic items (1)

- Raven's Advanced Progressive Matrices: A non-verbal test with diagrammatic items, in matrix form. Unlike the others, it can be used as a test of intellectual power alone, independent of speed (4, 6).

Tests of special aptitude or ability

From the early years of intelligence testing some psychologists considered that important information about an individual's ability was being obscured by concentrating on only one score, of general intelligence, and started looking at candidates' performance on specific types of items such as verbal or numerical questions (see Appendix 3). This trend was accelerated by Thurstone's identification of the seven primary mental abilities. For many years, test developers have concentrated their efforts on producing tests that measure and produce a single score for a specific mental ability, which is statistically reasonably independent of other special abilities. Such scores are not completely independent of each other because the influence of general intelligence also contributes to varying degrees – depending on the actual test – to a special ability score.

The terms 'special ability' or 'special aptitude' are often used imprecisely and interchangeably. A 'special aptitude' is a capacity for performing a specific group of tasks which have been shown statistically to be highly related to each other. The term 'special ability' is often used in the same sense, based upon its use in the theories of mental ability of both Thurstone and Vernon, where ability for special tasks is contrasted with general intellectual ability across all mental tasks. There are also aptitude tests for specific types of work, such as computer programming, which often combine different subtests of special abilities to provide an overall score which reflects the capacity to do a specific type of work. Some examples of aptitude tests for specific types of jobs are described below and are classified both by content, ie verbal, numerical, spatial, diagrammatic/symbolic – and by level, ie for lower-level and higher-level ability.

Examples of tests for special aptitude/ability

(a)   Verbal ability. There are a number of tests which measure lower levels of verbal (word) meaning and comprehension, some of which also necessitate an element of reasoning with words. All tests in this section have British norms:

- General Ability Test: Verbal (Source: 1)
- BST Literacy (2)
- Personnel Tests for Industry: Verbal (5)
- GAT Verbal Ability (2)
- MOST Word meanings (2)
- VC1 Verbal Evaluation (3)
- VP1 Verbal Usage (3).

Verbal tests involving significantly more complex mental operations of reasoning and critical evaluation are available for assessing candidates of high ability such as graduates and managers:

- Watson-Glaser Critical Thinking Appraisal Forms A and B (Source: 5); Form C, UK Edition (5, 6)
- CRT Verbal Skills (2)
- GMA Verbal Test (2)
- VMT1 Verbal Application (3)
- VMT3 Verbal Analysis (3)
- VMG1, 2 and 3 Verbal Critical Reasoning (3).

(b)   Numerical ability. Lower-level numerical tests often involve an understanding of, and skill at, arithmetical calculations and so candidates' existing attainments are being assessed as well as their aptitude:

- General Ability Test: Numerical (Source: 1)

- BST Numeracy (2)

- MOST Numerical Awareness and Estimation (2)

- GAT Numerical Ability (2)

- General Clerical Test – Numerical (5)

- NP2 and NTS2 Numerical Computation and Estimation (3)

- NP6 and NIT2 Numerical Reasoning (3)

- Personnel Tests for Industry – Numerical (5).

As with the verbal tests, there are also numerical tests for candidates of high ability such as graduates, and potential or actual supervisors and managers; these assess higher-order numerical reasoning and critical evaluation of quantitative information:

- CRT Numerical Skills (Source: 2)

- GMA Numerical Test (2)

- NMT4 Numerical Analysis (3)

- NC2 Interpreting Data (3)

- NMT2 Numerical Reasoning (3)

- NMG1, 2 and 3 Numerical Critical Reasoning (3).

(c) Spatial ability. Candidates are required to work mentally to identify, visualise, compare and/or manipulate two- or three-dimensional shapes. Such ability has a lower general intelligence component than many of the other abilities and is therefore a more distinct, purer ability.
   Tests for lower-level applicants include:

- Shapes Test (Source: 1)

- ET3 Visual Estimation (3)

- GAT Spatial Ability (2)

- ST8 Spatial Recognition (3).

Three tests for higher-ability candidates, which include three-dimensional shapes are:

- SIT7 Spatial Reasoning (Source: 3)
- STS5 Spatial Checking (3)
- Shapes Analysis Test (6).

(d) Diagrammatic ability. These tests do not include verbal or numerical items but include abstract symbols and diagrams, covering a range of operations from fairly superficial perceptual, to complex abstract, logical processes. Some designers argue that they are not dependent on attainment and so are purer measures of reasoning, but it is debatable whether they are 'culture free' or 'culture fair'. We will return to this complex argument later. Examples of lower-level diagrammatic tests are:

- DTS6 Diagrammatic Thinking (Source: 3)
- GAT Non-Verbal Ability (2)

The following tests are more appropriate for higher-ability candidates, such as technicians, scientists and software engineers:

- DIT6 Diagrammatic Reasoning (Source: 3)
- DIT5 Diagramming (3)
- GMA Abstract (2).

(e) Mechanical ability. This ability incorporates an element of intelligence and reasoning and is entirely separate from manual dexterity (see below). Inevitably, there is a knowledge component (elementary physics) and so the tests are not pure ability tests, but manuals do include evidence that they provide a measure of the capacity to learn and to succeed at certain jobs requiring mechanical ability and hence are tests of aptitude. Examples of mechanical aptitude tests are:

- Mechanical Ability Test (Source: 1)
- ACER Mechanical Reasoning (2)
- Bennett Mechanical Comprehension Tests (5, 6)
- MT4 Mechanical Comprehension (3).

(f) Manual dexterity. Eye–hand co-ordination is obviously relevant to

most manual tasks and research has shown that these abilities are not closely related to intelligence or to the abilities listed above. Indeed, there is a range of such fairly specific abilities requiring perception and manipulation involving fingers and hands. Some tasks require speed and little precision, whilst with others extreme precision is of paramount importance. Because such abilities are specific, it is necessary to carry out a careful analysis of the job before deciding on what test is most appropriate. Indeed, many successful tests are more akin to job samples or job simulations. However, some dexterity tests are available including the following:

- Stromberg Dexterity Test for testing arm–hand co-ordination (Source: 5)

- Bennett Hand Tool Dexterity Test, for assessing proficiency with conventional tools like spanners and screwdrivers (5)

- Crawford Small Parts Dexterity Test (5)

- Fine Dexterity Test (1, 6)

- Purdue Pegboard test, measuring two kinds of finger dexterity from gross movement to finger-tip dexterity (1)

- WSS Manual Dexterity, containing two tests of dexterity designed to assess fine and medium finger dexterity with mechanical objects (3).

- Manual Dexterity Test. A pencil-and-paper test designed to measure dexterity (Source: 1).

The Crawford and Fine Tests measure performance on precision tasks using small tools.

Examples of tests of aptitude for specific types of work/jobs

(a) Clerical speed and accuracy. For many lower-level office jobs, especially clerical jobs, an aptitude for identifying, comparing and checking similarities or differences of numerical, verbal or symbolic information is a requirement. This aptitude can also be one requirement of a few higher-level jobs as well, even though it is largely independent of general intelligence. There are a number of clerical tests available:

- Office Skills Speed and Accuracy Test (Source: 1)

- CP3 Checking (3)

- CP7 Basic Checking (3)

- CP8 Audio Checking (Oral Information) (3)

- GCT-R General Clerical Test (5).

There have, of course, been major changes in the nature of office work in recent years. The increased use of electronic equipment in the office of today has been shown to require higher-level checking and coding aptitudes. The following tests are relevant:

- CIT3 Computer Checking (Source: 3)

- CIT4 Syntax Checking (3)

- NE1 Numerical Estimation (3).

(b) Computer aptitude. Computer programming requires aptitudes to cope with the special forms of logical reasoning required. One tailor-made battery comprising five sub-tests which has been in use for over 25 years and is well validated across many different programming jobs is the:

- Computer Programmer Aptitude Battery (Source: 2).

A programming aptitude battery from various other batteries has been developed and validated, with different combinations of tests for different types of programming, systems analysis and software engineering. This is the:

- Information Technology Test Series (Source: 3).

The capacity for operating computer hardware is distinct from programming and two batteries have been developed and validated to assess this specific aptitude:

- Information System Skills (Source: 1)

- NTT Computer Commands; and Computer Rules (2).

(c) Language aptitude. The capacity to learn foreign languages is an aptitude that has been identified by research studies. The following test will probably be of interest to organisations that need to train staff to use a number of different foreign languages:

- Modern Languages Aptitude Test (Source: 5).

(d) Selling skills. Various tests have been devised specifically to assess the skills required primarily for lower-level sales and sales administration jobs. They are:

- Sales Profile (Source: 1)

- NS2 Reasoning with Data (3)

- VSI Using Written Information (3).

Test batteries
At the beginning of this chapter there was mention of batteries of tests comprising tests designed to be used together and which cover a wide range of special abilities and aptitudes for specific purposes.

Most of these have been referred to in the sections above. For selecting managers and graduates, there are the Advanced Test Battery from SHL and the Graduate and Management Battery from ASE; for apprentices and engineering technicians the Technical Test Battery from SHL; and for office staff the Personnel Test Battery from SHL. There are also differential ability batteries which are used widely for selection and which are particularly valuable for counselling purposes.

Differential batteries provide not only a score for each specific ability but also look at the relative scores of an individual across a profile to determine a person's relative strengths and weaknesses. Such batteries can be especially valuable for vocational guidance and counselling, and for placement purposes – allocating a person to a particular job from a choice of many to maximise his or her strengths, and the job–person match. Individual tests or combinations of tests from the batteries are often used for selection purposes. Of the differential batteries that cover a wide range of activities, the most widely used are:

- Differential Aptitude Tests (Source: 5)

- Morrisby Profile (1)

- General Abilities Profile (3).

Personality assessment and psychometric questionnaires

The term 'personality' is all-embracing in terms of the individual's

29

behaviour and the way it is organised and co-ordinated when he or she interacts with the environment. The sorts of personality characteristics which are normally assessed include emotional adjustment, social relations, motivation, interests, values and attitudes. However, some psychologists believe that cognitive processes (eg intelligence) should also be taken into account when looking at the total personality and so have included cognitive scales within their questionnaires.

While psychologists agree that specific aspects of an individual's personality, such as interests, motivations, values and attitudes are also relevant to occupational assessment and guidance, there are different views about how these aspects relate to one another. Some psychologists see them as overlapping to various degrees with an individual's personality. Others propose a hierarchical model, with personality traits at the bottom, influencing and determining values which in turn influence interests and motivations. These ultimately produce attitudes and a predisposition to behave in certain ways.

Within such a complex and wide-ranging field of study, there are obviously different theories of personality. Below there follow descriptions of the different methods of assessment, rather than descriptions of the theories themselves; for a brief account of the latter see Shackleton and Fletcher (1984).

Self-report personality questionnaires

These are of particular relevance to this book because the large majority of instruments used for occupational assessment of personality, motivations, interests, attitudes and values are self-report questionnaires. Furthermore, as already noted, some are available for use in the UK by non-psychologists provided that they are accredited users (see Chapter 2).

The foundations underlying personality questionnaires are the 'trait' or 'type' theories, which are closely related. The trait approach involves the identification of a number of fairly independent and enduring characteristics of behaviour which all people display, but to differing degrees. An example of such a trait is sociability, with a scale from extremely sociable to not sociable at all. Expressed in its simplest form, what trait theorists such as Cattell and Guilford have done is to identify examples of common behaviour, devise scales to measure these and then obtain ratings on these behaviours by people who know each other well. These observations have then been analysed statistically, using factor analysis, to generate broad traits to be found together, but which are fairly independent of other traits.

Groups of traits that are associated, but more loosely, go to make up personality 'types'.

Some of the words used to describe traits are also common in everyday language – examples are introvert and extravert, stable and anxious. When choosing and using questionnaires it is important to study the designer's definitions of the traits. Not only may there be important differences between the designer's definitions and those assumed by potential users, but there can also be differences in the way that the same terms have been defined by different designers. Certainly, traits with similar titles can reflect quite different behaviour. Accordingly, the author's definition of a particular trait must always be referred to in order to obtain a clear impression of what behaviour the trait actually represents. For example, the terms introversion and extraversion are used in a different sense in the MBTI from the way they are used by Cattell, Saville and most other psychologists in this field.

Questionnaires have been developed to measure these specific aspects of personality, and the choice of which instrument to use depends largely on the nature of the information users decide to be most relevant to their purposes and objectives.

The British Psychological Society (Bartram, 1995) has recently produced a detailed technical review of 30 personality or values questionnaires available in the UK. The general aims of this review are:

- to describe the principles of quality control

- to define standards for the evaluation of Level B instruments covering personality and values

- to provide fair and balanced evaluations to help users to judge their suitability for use in occupational assessment.

Ratings are given by two eminent psychologists in the field on the following attributes of each test: validity; reliability; quality of norms; quality of technical information available; clarity and coverage of content. In Section (iv) below we shall describe five of the most widely used instruments, all of which received favourable ratings across the five evaluation criteria, and which are all available to non-psychologists who have had Level B training. Space does not permit us to cover all 30 instruments, and readers are strongly recommended to refer to the BPS review if they wish to consider a wide range of potential instruments.

Personality questionnaires

(a) Cattell's 16 PF

The 16 Personality Factor questionnaire was developed nearly 50 years ago in the USA, initially for research and clinical purposes. However, for many years it has been used for general personality assessment and an enormous amount of research into its technical properties and its applications has been carried out. Detailed results are published in the 16 PF Handbook. A fifth edition (16PF5) has been published with UK norms, but the fourth edition is still available, also with British norms: Forms A and B, which are full versions, and C and D which are shorter versions, with simpler language for those with low educational attainment. All forms measure the same 16 primary factors and four second-order factors: introversion–extraversion; emotional stability; tough-poise; and independence. The test handbook also contains numerous empirically-derived indices of job-related criteria such as accident proneness, leadership, creativity and many others.

The questionnaire is used for both occupational assessment and counselling. All versions are untimed and take between 25 and 60 minutes to complete. (Sources: 2; industrial version, 6.)

(b) Gordon Personal Profile Inventory

This is a well-established instrument with much technical data contained within its manual. It has two parts. The Profile measures ascendancy, responsibility, emotional stability and sociability and the Inventory measures cautiousness, original thinking, personal relations and vigour. It is untimed, and each part usually takes 15–20 minutes to complete. It is useful for both counselling and assessment in an occupational setting. The norms in the manual are British and American (Sources: 2, 6.)

(c) Saville and Holdsworth's (SHL) Occupational Personality Questionnaire (OPQ®)

The OPQ® was published in 1984 after four years of systematic development in the UK. It is designed specifically to assess personality characteristics in the world of work for assessment and counselling purposes. There are eight different versions, with various response formats used in each version. Therefore, some are more suitable for selection purposes, others for counselling. The main domains of personality measured by the OPQ® are: relationships with people; thinking style; and feelings and emotions. The longest form, Concept Model

4.2, assesses 30 primary factors and takes about 50 minutes to complete, whilst the shortest, Images, measures six dimensions and takes about 10 minutes. The manual contains British norms for all versions. Managerial and professional, and graduate and general population norms are available for different versions. Extensive reliability data on all versions are presented. Supplements to the manual, covering additional norms and research data are produced on a regular basis. A detailed report of numerous validation study results is available. Some versions have been translated into a number of different European languages as well as Japanese and Chinese. (Source: 3.)

(d) Myers-Briggs Type Indicator®

This American personality questionnaire has been developed over the last 35 years and is based on Jung's theory of types. It contains four scales: introversion-extraversion; sensing-intuition; thinking-feeling; and judging-perceptive. Scores can be reported as continuous variables or as a specific type code. There are two British versions, Form K and a shorter Form G, which are both untimed and usually take around 30 and 20 minutes respectively to complete. The Indicator is used primarily in personal counselling, although there is also limited evidence of its value as a selection aid. The manual contains UK norms for interpretations. (Source: 4.)

(e) Californian Psychological Inventory

This questionnaire was also developed in the USA and a large number of research studies have been carried out over the last 40 years. It is designed to assess personality characteristics that are relevant for everyday life and the revised edition measures five basic scales: interpersonal style and manner; internalisation and endorsement of normative conventions; thinking and behaviour; cognitive and intellectual functioning; and special scales such as managerial, creative and leadership potential. The two versions contain 309 and 434 items and usually take between 45 and 60 minutes to complete. British editions are now available with UK norms. A guide to interpretation and a CPI handbook are also available. (Source: 4.)

Interest questionnaires

These have usually been designed for vocational and career guidance purposes, although most instruments have been used for selection purposes with some positive results. They are designed for use with teenagers and adults.

(a) Strong Interest Inventory

This American questionnaire which has been developed over the last 50 years has just been revised and surveys attitudes to a large number of different jobs. Responses are compared with successful men and women in a wide range of occupations, and scores are produced for six general themes, 25 basic interest scores (eg public speaking) and 207 occupational scores. The questionnaire takes 15 to 30 minutes to complete. A manual and user's guide are available, containing American data. (Source: 4.)

(b) Rothwell-Miller Interest Blank

This questionnaire was first published in Australia in 1958; a British edition was published in 1968 with UK data. There are two versions of the questionnaire, one for male and one for female subjects, who rank occupations which represent 12 general areas of interest. The results reflect respondents' preferences for particular types of occupations. It is primarily a counselling instrument but is also used for selection (especially apprentice) and placement purposes. It takes about 20 minutes to complete. Revised and unisex versions are now available (Source: 1.)

(c) Guilford-Zimmerman Interest Inventory

This American inventory is self-administered, takes about 20 minutes to complete and measures 10 scales – natural; mechanical; scientific; creativity; literary; artistic; service; enterprising; leadership and clerical. It reports the individual's interests as related to major vocations and pastimes. It can be used for a general assessment of work-related interests and for individual–job matching. A manual contains information on reliability and validity, and normative data from the USA. (Source: 4.)

(d) SHL General Occupational Interest Inventory

This British questionnaire is designed for those with low or no formal educational qualifications and takes about 35 minutes to complete. Individuals state whether they like a number of activities related to specific jobs. Eighteen scores are provided, including people, office, control, leisure and practical. The manual provides British standardisation data. The Inventory is used primarily for counselling but also for selection and placement (Source: 3.)

(e) SHL Advanced Occupational Interest Inventory

This British questionnaire, designed for adolescents with GCSEs and above, is also used for employees in graduate and management positions.

There is no time limit but it normally takes about 35 minutes to complete. Respondents provide their preferences for a number of relevant job activities and scores are produced on 19 categories of interests. The three main domains are people, data and practical interests. UK norms are provided in the manual and the inventory is used primarily for counselling, but also for selection and placement. (Source: 3.)

(f)   SHL Management Interest Inventory

This British inventory is designed for people currently in, or likely to rise to, management grades. There is no time limit but it normally takes about 30 minutes to complete. Subjects provide information on their experience of various skills and functions and their liking of specific relevant activities. Scores are produced on 12 management functions (eg sales, finance, data processing) and on 12 management skills (eg problem-solving, decision-making, organising and communicating). The inventory is used for counselling, selection and placement purposes and the manual contains UK normative data. (Source: 3.)

Values questionnaires

Gordon Surveys of Values (Personal and Interpersonal)

Each of the two surveys covers six values – *Interpersonal:* support, conformity, recognition, independence, benevolence and leadership. *Personal:* practical-mindedness, achievement, variety, decisiveness, orderliness and goal-orientation. They are untimed but usually take about 10 minutes each. The Surveys in the UK are used more for employment purposes than for counselling. The manual is American but UK norms are available. (Source: 2.)

Specific sales behaviour questionnaires

Two questionnaires are available which cover specific work behaviour within the broad personality domain. The two examples described below are quite widely used in the UK and have sound validity evidence within their manuals.

(a)   Poppleton-Allen Sales Aptitude Test (PASAT)

Although this is described as an aptitude test, it is a self-report questionnaire of 'habitual responses' rather than a test of 'maximum response' and so is included in this section. It is designed to measure 15 different sales behaviours and is based upon quite extensive job analysis and factor analytic research on sales staff in the late 1970s. The job behaviour factors cover the areas of social skills, organisation and planning, emotional expression and motivation. It is untimed but usually takes 20–30 minutes to complete. It is designed specifically for selection of applicants for sales jobs. The manual contains British norms for different types of selling and other technical data. (Source: 6.)

(b) Customer Contact Questionnaire (CCQ)
This is designed to measure 16 dimensions of personality relevant for non-supervisory staff working in sales or customer service roles. Version 7.2 is forced choice, while 5.2 is a normative version, with 136 questions. Relevant UK norms are available (Source: 3.)

Other approaches to the assessment of personality

(a) Simulation/situational tests
One method of assessing personality which is used quite widely is the use of trained assessors to evaluate clearly-defined personality characteristics which are described in behavioural terms so that each assessor is looking for exactly the same qualities (eg assertiveness, flexibility, stress tolerance). Assessors watch candidates attempt situational exercises which simulate work at the level at which candidates will be expected to perform in the organisation. This approach often forms part of an Assessment Centre, at which candidates are also assessed by other means including interviews and psychological tests. Further details of assessment centres and other methods appear in Chapter 11.

(b) Projective techniques
Each candidate is presented with a relatively unstructured task of stimuli which provide wide latitude in terms of response. The assumption underlying such methods is that the candidate will 'project' his or her attitudes, values, motivations and so on into responses to the ambiguous material. These methods have sometimes been effective if used alongside an interview by psychologists with special training. They have the specific advantage that they are disguised in their purpose and so it is very difficult for the subject to present a false favourable image or desired impression. Techniques such as sentence completion, the Rorschach 'inkblots' and the Thematic Apperception Test (TAT) have been used in personnel assessment with some evidence of success but they do pose questions about reliability and validity, and there are often major problems about face validity, ie acceptability to candidates,

especially questions of relevance. Projective tests are not available to non-psychologists and anyone who wishes to try them out is advised to approach only psychologists with extensive experience of their use in the occupational assessment field.

(c) Objective tests of personality

Some psychologists, notably Cattell, have devised experimental laboratory situations to test the hypothesis that psycho-physiological measures, eg heart rate, respiration rate, brain wave patterns, are correlates of personality characteristics. These tests involve either giving subjects a specific task to perform or subjecting them to some kind of specific stimulus, such as the sound of a gun shot, and measuring changes in psycho-physiological patterns. Whilst there is limited evidence that, for example, introverts and extraverts behave differently in some of these test situations, the evidence is not strong, and there are major problems in terms of acceptability to subjects! Such methods have not been used in occupational assessment in the UK, although the polygraph (lie-detector), which is a variant of such psycho-physiological assessment methods, has been introduced recently by a few organisations. Its use has, however, been strongly criticised by The British Psychological Society. Again, such methods are beyond the scope of this book.

(d) Fringe methods of personality assessment

The resurgence of interest in scientific personality assessment has also brought in its wake interest in non-scientific methods such as handwriting analysis (graphology), astrology, palmistry, phrenology and so on. A study by Robertson and Makin (1986) showed that 2.6 per cent of the top 1,000 UK companies always used graphology when assessing managers. Yet a major review of the effectiveness of the method by Klimoski and Rafaeli (1983) concluded, in studies which have been scientifically rigorous, that the results have not supported the usefulness of inferences based on handwriting. They concluded, 'given the evidence that we do have a great reliance on inferences based on script must be considered unwarranted'.

Summary

The purpose of this chapter has been briefly to describe mental abilities and personality, to outline how they can be assessed and to give brief details of some of the better known tests that are available.

It must again be stressed that this is not a comprehensive list, that the illustrative descriptions are not an endorsement of the tests, and that technical qualities and relevance to particular circumstances must be carefully assessed.

3
Ethical, legal and social issues

This chapter begins with a description of possible criteria for determining whether or not testing is ethical; it goes on to compare these criteria with guidelines from two relevant professional bodies – The British Psychological Society and the Institute of Personnel and Development. Next there is discussion of the legal aspects of testing. Finally there is discussion about social issues associated with the use of tests.

Criteria for determining whether testing is ethical

People who are new to the topic of psychological testing often ask for recommendations about a 'good' test. In the previous chapter we have referred to tests that are generally regarded as being 'good' tests in so far as they have been relatively well designed from a technical point of view and have been shown to be effective at measuring what they claim to measure.

However, if testing is to be fully effective from the point of view of both the tester and the person being tested, the technical features of the test are only a part of what needs to be considered. In an ideal world it might be argued that a test or tests would be used only under the following circumstances:

1 The test has been well-designed from a technical point of view; this would include meeting technical standards in terms of reliability and validity (see Chapter 2) and being shown to avoid unfair discrimination in terms of sex, race or disability.

2 The test is used only in circumstances where its worth has been proven.

3 Those administering, scoring, and interpreting the test scores are trained to appropriate standards; this would include people who work with computers to develop expert systems which 'write' narrative reports based on test scores.

4 Those being tested know why they are being asked to take the tests.

5 Those being tested are given information such as a test description handout prior to testing to give examples of questions and/or practice questions.

6 Testing is in accordance with the test designer's recommendations in an environment that will enable those being tested to give of their best.

7 Test results are scored accurately.

8 Test results are interpreted accurately; this includes interpretation by narrative reports which are generated by feeding test results into computers.

9 Test results are available to those who have been tested, and they can be given 'feedback' about the results and their implications.

10 Records of test scores and their implications remain available to those who have been tested.

11 Records of test scores are used appropriately.

12 All the above processes are monitored and evaluated to check their worth and to make improvements where possible.

In practice it would be rare for testing to fully satisfy all twelve conditions listed above. Some of the reasons for falling short of the ideal are detailed below.

1 Technical standards

One sign of a 'good' test is that it is supported by information about reliability, validity and fairness. However, there are also two potential problems. One is that information about these characteristics is often presented in the form of statistics and many potential test purchasers do not have sufficient understanding of statistics to know what the figures mean. The second is that there are no 'absolute' standards for test design, and acceptability may be a matter of professional or legal interpretation.

2 Restricting use to situations of proven worth

It might be argued that the use of tests should be confined to situations where their worth had been clearly demonstrated. However, at least two potential problems arise. First, the costs of bringing a test to market would be greatly increased if the worth of the test had to be fully proven before it was released, and in practice this would restrict the freedom of choice of test purchasers and users. Second, many factors combine to determine the success of testing including the applicants tested, the work to be done, and the training given; it is unlikely that all these factors will be exactly the same in a new situation.

It is not unknown for tests to be used on a speculative basis – for example, to see whether or not they might give insight into a particular situation, such as understanding why a team of managers does not appear to be operating to its full potential. Under these circumstances, 'feedback' is likely to focus on the test or tests which appear to give insight and understanding about the behaviour of the group, rather than tests which do not.

3   Using specially trained staff

Five levels of training can be identified.

One is the level of training required to administer tests; this involves setting out the room to be used for testing, introducing the tests, and answering any questions raised by those being tested. Accurate timing is important if psychometric tests are to be used properly. The role of the test administrator may also involve marking (but not interpreting) the tests. Some test administrators attend formal training courses, have their skills assessed and are 'registered' by the course provider; others may be trained 'on the job' by a test user.

A second level is the level of training required to interpret specific tests. People trained to this level will have attended a training course run by a test supplier, and will have been registered by the supplier. Courses of this kind are tending to be replaced by the third level of course.

The third level is the level of training required for the Certificate of Competence in Psychological Testing at Level A; this indicates an understanding of psychometric tests (ie tests of attainment, general intelligence, or special ability or aptitude) to a level which The British Psychological Society considers to be consistent with sound practice.

The fourth and fifth levels refer to the Certificate in Competence in Psychological Testing at Level B for Psychometric Questionnaires (ie questionnaires measuring personality, interests or values); these certificates are relatively new and, at present, only qualified and experienced chartered psychologists have full Level B certificates (ie level 5). (The certificates of competency are discussed in more detail in the next chapter).

In practice there is a tendency for people to claim to be trained (when they are not) or for them to claim to be trained to a higher level than is in fact the case. Sometimes the individual is making the claim, but sometimes organisations will ask individuals to do work beyond the scope of their formal training; sometimes the individual and the organisation conspire to claim a higher level of training than really exists so as to give credibility and/or try to save time or money.

4 Explaining the reasons for testing

It is reasonable to expect that people who are being tested will be told why they are being asked to take tests and what use will be made of the test results. Research and experience both suggest that some of the most adverse reactions to testing amongst candidates are caused by lack of information and knowledge about the tests and the way they are being used. To create the right conditions for testing and to ensure that candidates are appropriately briefed, the following steps need to be taken:

● The candidates need to understand the *place* of tests in the selection procedure. This means offering some information on how they will be used and on what influence they will have – what weight will be given to them in terms of the whole selection process. Silvester and Brown (1993) found that candidates believed – in the absence of any information – that too much reliance was being placed on test results; candidates will probably feel more positive if they know that the tests are not normally a pass/fail type of hurdle. Where some of the more common tests are administered, it is perhaps important to indicate that they may be used in different ways (and have different norms) by different organisations.

● The candidates need to be able to see the *relevance* of the tests to the job requirements; in other words, the tests need face validity. (Lounsbury *et al* 1989; Rynes and Connerly, 1993)

● The candidates need to be assured of the *accuracy* or validity of the measures (Rynes and Connerly, 1993) and, by implication, that there is a lack of bias.

● They need to be assured of the *competence* of those using the tests and interpreting the results; a good test can still be rendered worthless by incorrect application or interpretation. Having the BPS Level A and B statements of competence is obviously relevant here. (See also below under Interpretation).

Quite apart from the use of tests in the context of the specific selection procedure, there is the possibility of them being referred to later in other situations. Within organisations, people who apply for one post and who

42

are unsuccessful may have their test scores and other information passed to other managers. This may be done with the best of intentions, but candidates should none the less be assured that their permission will be sought before such information is passed on.

More sinister, in terms of being told the use to which test data will be put, is the practice of inviting individuals to take tests as part of a 'development centre' when the reality is that those who do not reach required standards will find themselves without work and being made redundant. Similarly, some organisations may retain external consultants to administer tests as part of 'career counselling' or 'career development' but may then ask the consultants for reports and use this information to make decisions about the future of those who have been tested.

5 Giving information in advance of testing

If an individual has had little or no experience of being tested, his or her initial test results may not be accurate. For example, if a reasoning test with a choice of answers is being taken for the first time, the person being tested may be confused by one or more of the features of the test, such as:

- being given a choice of answers and needing to identify the 'correct' one

- how to record the answers

- knowing what balance to strike between working quickly and working accurately.

Also, there may also be some confusion among those taking a personality questionnaire for the first time. They may worry excessively about whether they should answer 'Yes' or 'No' to an individual item because they feel they are mainly in the middle, without understanding that any one item will be of very limited significance in terms of the overall scores obtained. Actually, there is quite a strong argument for saying that as part of the information given in advance of testing, some simple background should be provided on how tests are constructed. This helps candidates understand them much better and takes away some of the mistaken beliefs and 'mythology' that surround tests and which can cause apprehension about them.

Information in the form of 'test description handouts' can help people to make appropriate responses; there is evidence that such handouts can also play an important part in avoiding unfair discrimination (see below).

6 The testing environment

So far as psychometric tests are concerned, scores can be maximised by a test environment in which there is an atmosphere of 'quiet urgency'; lower scores may be obtained by an inappropriate atmosphere (eg too 'laid back' or too much tension or anxiety) or by other environmental problems (eg heat, cold, noise etc).

7 Accurate scoring

Scoring may be inaccurate for a number of reasons. For example, when psychometric tests are being marked the wrong answer key may be used (ie the respondents replies 'marked' by comparison with incorrect – rather than correct – answers); other possibilities are that test scores may be incorrectly totalled, or that errors may be made in transferring an individual's test score on to a summary sheet or other documentation, or into reports.

8 Interpretation

Errors can occur in the interpretation of tests and questionnaires. For example, an individual's score on a test (often the number of correct answers) may be compared with the wrong norms – norms are the scores of others who have already taken the test. For example, the same score may look high if compared with a norm group of 16-year-old school-leavers, but low if compared with a group of top managers with business qualifications.

Use of inappropriate norms can also lead to errors in the interpretation of personality questionnaires. There can be other errors, too. For example, in one widely used personality questionnaire, individuals are asked a number of questions about whether they enjoy working with figures; this can sometimes be erroneously interpreted as an indication of *ability* to work with numbers rather than a *preference* for working with numbers; while preference may be affected by ability so far as some individuals are concerned, one does not always predict the other; the difference between 'ability' and 'preference' can be really important.

Errors of interpretation may reflect a lack of understanding on the part of the person using the test, or may reflect the way that the results have been expressed in writing; for example, there is sometimes a wish to 'dramatise' the findings in order to make the comparisons between different applicants more vivid. These kinds of errors are not confined to individuals; they can also be found in many computer-generated reports.

9   Giving feedback

Feedback can be important to people taking tests for a number of reasons. If people are taking tests as part of a selection procedure and are unsuccessful, knowledge of their test results can help them to decide what to do next; for example, if they learn that they reached the required standard but that the vacancy has been offered to an even stronger candidate, they may decide to apply again in the future; if they learn that they are just below the required standard, they may decide to prepare for a future selection procedure and to apply again when they are ready; if they learn that they are well below the required standard they may decide to stop applying for the same or similar work and to look for alternatives. However, all these decisions require that 'feedback' is given to the individual, and it is still rare for organisations to give such feedback to all the applicants that are tested.

The evidence is clear (Iles and Roberston 1995; Lounsbury et al 1989) that providing feedback is linked to more favourable attitudes to test use. But perhaps it is not just a question of simply giving feedback; elements of organisational justice theory suggest that it is important for candidates to have the opportunity to correct what they believe are erroneous impressions formed of them. Actually, this seldom happens in the UK, as most feedback is made post-selection decision. In Holland the ethical code for psychologists makes it clear that candidates may require that the results of tests be presented to them before anyone else (de Wolff, 1989).

10   Availability of records of testing

Records of testing are not always available to the individuals who have been tested after initial decisions have been made. Sometimes the individuals would like to refer back to them – for example, a personality profile may be administered as part of a selection procedure; at a later stage an individual who was tested may ask to see the profile again – if successful as an aid to thinking about their development needs in the new job, if unsuccessful as an aid to thinking about what to next.

11   Appropriate use of records of testing

This relates back to the point made earlier about giving assurances on how test results will be used beyond the situation where they were obtained in the first place. Records of testing may not always be used appropriately. For example, some managers might try to make decisions on the basis of testing which took place months or even years earlier – in the intervening time individuals may have changed considerably, perhaps enhancing their skills or even having declining skills because of lack of practice or health or other problems. While the best tests can provide well-constructed measures of aspects of individuals at a point in time, this does not preclude a degree of subsequent change and development, especially (a) with younger candidates and (b) in the personality domain.

12 Monitoring, evaluating and improving

Because of the large number of factors that can affect the success of testing, and the selection and other procedures of which testing may be part, it is important that testing programmes are monitored and evaluated regularly.

Later chapters of this book indicate how such reviews may be carried out; however, the statistical and other skills required mean that most readers will need to take professional advice from reputable test suppliers or independent chartered psychologists.

Standards laid down by professional bodies

Two professional bodies with significant interests in testing are:

- The British Psychological Society
- the Institute of Personnel and Development.

The British Psychological Society's Steering Committee on Test Standards has published *Psychological Testing – A User's Guide*. The guide is organised into four sections:

- what to look for in a psychological test
- what qualifies as competence in the use of psychological tests
- a commitment to responsible use of psychological tests
- further information.

In discussing the responsible use of tests, the guide identifies the following parties:

- the test developer
- the test supplier
- the test user

- the candidate
- the client (who may be one of the above, but may be a third party).

The guide proposes a set of questions as a means by which each party can contribute to the responsible use of psychological tests; together, the questions and their answers should meet the following requirements:

- that the purpose of testing is clearly stated and communicated to all parties involved in the testing process
- that the procedures for testing are clearly stated and communicated to all parties involved in the testing process
- that it is clear how the test information will be used and communicated to all parties in the testing process
- that procedures for dealing with enquiries and complaints about the process of testing are clearly stated and communicated to all parties involved in the testing process.

The Institute of Personnel and Development published a *Guide on Psychological Testing* in 1997 (IPD 1997); this replaced the *Code on Occupational Testing* first published in 1988. The guide aims to ensure that:

- proper consideration is given to the appropriateness of using tests
- tests are used in a professional manner which is relevant to the employment context
- equality of opportunity is ensured throughout the process
- test results are scored, interpreted, evaluated and communicated by appropriately trained individuals
- individuals taking tests are informed of the reasons for the test and the conditions under which it will be used, how the information will be used and stored, and are given the opportunity to receive feedback on the test results.

Legal aspect of testing

Current legislation regarding unfair discrimination in the use of tests concerns

- sex discrimination

- racial discrimination

- disability discrimination.

It is possible that further legislation will be introduced in the future (eg to avoid unfair discrimination on the grounds of age). In addition, test materials are subject to legislation regarding copyright, while the storage of test scores on computers is subject to the Data Protection Act 1984.

Avoiding unfair discrimination

There are two kinds of discrimination. One, *direct discrimination*, means that applicants are treated unfavourably because of their sex, their ethnic origin or their disability. The other kind of discrimination, *indirect discrimination*, is the result of using a selection method which disadvantages some groups. Testing can be a source of indirect discrimination, even though the testing programme may have been introduced with the best of intentions. The unfair discrimination can be caused by the tests themselves, or by the way that the tests are being used.

When choosing tests, the ideal would be for test purchasers to be able to choose from a wide variety of tests which do not discriminate unfairly, but in practice it is very difficult to develop such tests. One reason is that it is generally acknowledged that every individual's environmental and cultural background will affect his or her test performance. The greater the difference between the individual's background and the norm for the culture in which the tests have been developed and used, the greater the possibility of unfair discrimination.

Studies involving the large-scale use of tests have found that many tests show measurable differences in the test scores and profiles of males when compared to females and of groups of people of different ethnic backgrounds. These differences can often be shown to be statistically significant. However, statistical significance depends on *both* the numbers of people in the studies *and* the size of the difference between the scores of the two groups. Because the numbers of people in the studies are often large, the differences in the scores may be (and often are) small and there is always considerable overlap between the different groups or populations. Debate has therefore centred on four issues:

- First, have 'real' differences in test scores been found or could these be the result of errors in sampling or in the choice or use of statistics etc?

- Second, do any differences that are found reflect differences in the education, experience, opportunity or values of the different groups?

- Third, do any differences found suggest differences between the two groups of a kind that might be related to inherited qualities such as genetic factors?

- Fourth, if differences have been found, can the test be used in a selection procedure if it seems appropriate in other ways?

Whatever the origins of the differences in the test scores, it is often possible to minimise the chances of unfair discrimination when choosing a test. Check the technical manual supplied with the test (all good tests will have a technical manual or equivalent document) to see whether the test performance of subgroups (eg men and women, or members of different ethnic groups) has been investigated and reported. If the evidence is available and indicates that the test does not discriminate unfairly, this should be regarded as a positive feature. However, it should not lead to complacency; when using tests, always make arrangements to monitor their use for the possibility of unfair discrimination.

Careful monitoring is particularly important if relevant evidence is not available (as may be the case for a test which is still being developed, or for a few older tests developed before the mid-1970s) or if there is already some unfavourable evidence about a test which is being used because it clearly reflects the requirements of the job and/or has a number of other features in its favour.

Given a situation in which tests may discriminate unfairly, there are several practical points which may make the testing as a whole more acceptable to candidates and which may minimise any unfair discrimination:

- Ensure that both the content of the test and the instructions for completing the test are directly relevant to the vacancies; for example, the use of a test with complex written instructions cannot be justified for a vacancy in which there is little written work to be done; without changes to the instructions, it is likely that the testing would unfairly discriminate against those whose command of written English would be sufficient to do the job.

- Provide test description handouts or example sheets which describe the tests and the reasons for using them, and which give examples of sample questions for the applicants to try; there is evidence to suggest that these approaches will have the greatest benefit if applicants are encouraged to do some practice questions, rather than simply read about them and/or look at some completed examples. When tests are to be completed against time limits it can be advantageous to complete the practice examples against time limits too.

- Ensure that the tests being used contain practice examples which the applicants can try immediately before they start the test; candidates from some ethnic groups or social classes may well be apprehensive when faced with tests; untimed example sessions immediately before testing starts can help to reduce nervousness and unfamiliarity with testing still further, ensuring that when testing starts all the candidates are ready to give of their best.

In the final analysis, tests that discriminate unfairly can be used in selection if they can be shown to predict work performance. Experience suggests that tests which reflect the content of the workplace are less likely to be challenged than those which do not. However, we would hope that progressive employers would not be satisfied with any situation involving discrimination even if their actions were defensible at law; such employers might be willing to provide alternative entry routes, to place more emphasis on training and less on selection, and so on.

Testing and disability

Since the Disability Discrimination Act (1995) is fairly new, it is worth saying a little more specifically on this topic. The Act is accompanied by a code of practice to help employers to comply with their new duties under the Act; the code is not law but must be taken into account by a Court or Tribunal when determining any relevant question. Paragraph 5.12 of the code gives advice on carrying out aptitude and other tests. The code indicates that aptitude and other tests can be carried out in the recruitment process where the nature and form of the test are necessary to assess a matter relevant to the job. It goes on to give two illustrations of where the use of a test might be called into question:

- The first illustration concerns the use of a numeracy test where the job entails very little numeracy work; it suggests that the requirement for a disabled person to pass the test might be waived.

- The second illustration concerns the use of a short oral test; it is suggested that adjustments might be made (eg more time to complete the test, or give the test in written form instead) if oral communication is not relevant to the job.

Both illustrations seem to us to raise the question of why inappropriate tests were being given to applicants (whether disabled or not) rather than to give any profound insight into how to avoid unfair discrimination against disabled people.

Clearly, though, the job analysis has to be scrutinised particularly closely in the context of disability. It is the case that disabled people may tackle a job in a slightly different manner to others, but with equal effectiveness. Thus, the need is to review what genuinely *is* essential, rather than just desirable, in terms of the job analysis and person-specification. None the less, if for example, a valid selection measure indicates that a person cannot assimilate and use numerical information at a speed that will be necessary to do the job effectively, then the candidate's performance on that measure – whether due to disability or not – can justifiably be used in making the selection decision. Where care has to be taken is in ensuring that performance in selection is going to be typical of performance in the job; disabled candidates may benefit more than most from being given some practice in dealing with assessment methods that they have not encountered before.

Another issue is the substitution of one assessment method for another to get round the problem posed by a particular disability. For example, if the normal way of assessing achievement orientation is by interview, this could be difficult to apply in the case of a deaf candidate. It may be better to use an appropriate personality questionnaire as an alternative way of getting information on this quality in such a case. Where tests are used, every effort needs to be made to ascertain the nature and extent of the individual's disability before the testing session, so that suitable arrangements can be made. A few general pointers are:

- For people with hearing disabilities it will be important to have written test instructions rather than presenting these orally. Communicating starting and stopping times will need to be done through visual or tactile means. Questions from the candidate about the test can either be dealt with in writing or – if available – by sign language.

- For people with visual disabilities, administering tests can represent greater difficulty. In some cases, the individual does have a degree of vision, and may be able to take tests with the aid of magnifiers or if given large-print versions of the tests. In other cases, Braille versions of tests may be necessary; however, increasingly, computer-based voice simulation is used by this group. Audio tapes or oral presentation of the test content and candidate responses is another alternative. At the time of writing, few of the main test producers have a suite of tests in Braille and/or large-print format; some of these are slightly older versions of the tests currently being marketed. It is important to remember that whatever method is used to assist candidates with reading the tests has also to apply to their use of answer sheets.

- It is difficult to specify general advice for people with other disabilities. Candidates with dyslexia will need more time to read the materials, some candidates with motor disorders may find it helpful to have enlarged answer sheets, and so on.

In terms of interpretation, people with disabilities may need longer to complete tests than is normally allowed (and the time needed for giving the instructions beforehand may also be greater); this has to be determined on a case-by-case basis. Moreover, their performance on the tests – especially ability measures – cannot be compared in a straightforward way with the standard norm groups, if only because they have frequently taken the tests under slightly different conditions. The small numbers of disabled candidates precludes the development of separate norms for them, so the best advice is to use the normal norm tables, but to interpret them in the light of the likelihood of there being more error in the measurement than is normally the case. So, the 'true' test score might vary more around the score actually obtained to a greater degree than we would expect with other candidates. This means that test scores should be considered only as approximations, and should be looked at carefully in the context of other assessment data, including the candidate's previous record of achievement.

More detailed advice on testing people with disabilities is outside the scope of this general guide for managers but is available from reputable test suppliers, and an excellent guide is published by at least one of the major test suppliers, Saville and Holdsworth Ltd.

Social issues associated with the use of tests

Elsewhere in this book we have painted a positive picture of the use of tests. At their best they benefit both employers (who are able to identify potentially productive employees) and the employees who are placed in types of work where they can maximise their output and earnings.

Many of the problems that arise from the use of tests are a result of the misuse of the tests. As psychologists we are disappointed that accounts of the misuse often make reference to 'psychological tests' when the advice of psychologists has either not been taken or has even been ignored.

In theory, individuals can seek redress if they are unfairly adversely affected by testing. However, in practice such actions are stressful for the individual as well as being costly and time consuming. Individuals may also feel that they will be branded as being potential trouble-makers, and that no financial award can really compensate for what has been, and what will be, involved.

A particular problem concerns the collection of information about 'suspect' tests, ie those for which there is little or no evidence of technical worth. It could be argued that it would be helpful for British law to be changed to accommodate 'group actions'; the work of a chartered psychologist could then form part of legal action taken on behalf of a large number of people who felt that they had been treated unfairly by the use of a test, rather then focusing on a particular situation or employer.

There remains the issue of the impact of tests even if they were used according to best ethical practice. Would we then have some kind of Utopian situation at work ? Our views are that:

- tests will always have limitations

- different opinions will remain

- wider social issues need to be considered.

Limitations of testing

Individual performance at work always has a number of elements. Even for relatively straightforward jobs there are a number of elements, such as the quality and quantity of output, ease or difficulty of supervision, relationships at work, timekeeping and attendance. For more complex jobs there are issues such as strategic thinking, relationships with customers, organisational skills, efficiency and effectiveness. In addition there are issues for all employees around motivation and ambition. It is rare for an individual employee to be consistently good (or consistently poor) at all features of their work, rather, people tend to perform well in some areas and less well in others.

Individual tests cannot be expected to predict all elements of performance. Accordingly, they should never be used for selection on their own, and even combinations of tests have limitations in predicting all aspects of performance at work. Arguably the best indicator of performance at work is a sample of performance of work (eg performance during a trial period) but even this has limitations because people differ in their ability and interest in developing to meet future job requirements.

Different opinions

At the end of an assessment procedure involving the use of tests, most candidates are seen to have some positive features, and most have some negative features too. In spite of careful preparation and agreement about what will be assessed and why, there can be differences of opinion about the importance of differences in test scores, the relative importance of different tests and other information.

Particular debate may centre around the differences in style that can be accommodated in a particular role, and the extent to which an individual may be able to adapt. For example, one successful strategic director in a large organisation became 'stuck' at its lower levels because his somewhat cerebral approach was seen to be far better suited to strategic headquarters than to the operational side of the business; however, he realised that without the operational experience his future career would be severely limited. He obtained the operational experience that he required at his thirteenth attempt.

In general, assessment procedures do seem to be helping some people to identify their strongest abilities and to put them to good use early in their careers. However, they may be less successful in helping people to leave behind their proven skills and abilities and to take on responsibilities in new areas. Thus people may feel trapped in areas of work in which they are proficient but increasingly bored.

Wider social issues

Throughout this chapter we have repeated that, in the eyes of the law, unfair discrimination is avoided if the contents of tests reflect the content of work to be done. This will mean that tests are likely to become more, rather than less, job related. In turn, those who can learn about the content of the work to be done in advance of the selection procedure are likely to do better than those who are unable to do so.

Unless those responsible for testing make fairness a priority, testing may favour the better educated and the better informed. For example, ability tests that are administered by computer may be done better by those familiar with computers (because they or their school could afford them) than those who have little of no prior experience.

Some may be content that this is the case, and that investment in education and individual study and effort are being rewarded. Others may wish to reflect on the experiences of the British Army in the Second World War. At one stage, potential officers were selected by interview. Toplis and Stewart (1983) describe details given in a 1942 edition of the magazine *Picture Post*:

> A man who showed promise in his unit was recommended to the CO [commanding officer] for interview. On the strength of the interviewer's impression in a fifteen-minute talk, the candidate was either rejected or sent on a course at the OCTU (officer cadet training unit). Stories got around that it was no good putting up for commission unless you'd won your colours at cricket and rode to hounds.

For this reasons, the numbers wanting to be officers had virtually dried up in the middle of war. Worse still, half the candidates recommended for commission proved unsuitable to become officers when tested in actual training. Alarmed Members of Parliament learned what was happening and asked questions in the House of Commons.

A new approach to selection was taken when War Office Selection Boards were set up. Garforth, a professional soldier, described the methods used:

> Tests may vary from a 'group discussion', in which eight or ten candidates sit round in easy chairs and are told to select a subject for discussion and talk about it to each other, to a 'group task' which may involve improvising, with limited materials found on the spot, some method of 'escaping' as a group over a wire entanglement, including electrified wire and alarms. In another form of the test, groups are told to invent their own situations and act on them.

These methods were added to other methods of selection (such as individual interviews, intelligence and other tests, and medical examinations) to assess the subject's ability to get on with, and influence, his colleagues, to display qualities of spontaneous leadership and to think and produce ideas in a real-life situation.

The *Picture Post* article reported that, since the new boards had been set up, the numbers of men applying for commissions had doubled. After the war the general approach of the boards was copied by the British Civil Service and by commercial organisations on both sides of the Atlantic.

Testing and other selection methods do not have to favour the better educated and better informed; whether they do so is currently a matter for the designers of selection methods and the employers who use them; ultimately government must decide whether legislation is required.

Summary

The way that tests are chosen and used can have important implications for those taking the tests, those administering them, existing employees, the local community and even society as a whole. The impact of testing can range from the success with which individual appointments are made to affecting the image of the organisation as an employer – what some have called the 'employer brand'; in turn this can affect employee satisfaction and ultimately commercial and other success.

4
Obtaining tests: Certificates of competence

As mentioned in Chapter 1, properly designed psychological tests are supplied only to people who have appropriate training. Accordingly, managers or others who wish to introduce tests, or widen the range of tests being used, have to consider how this might best be done. In practice, there are four main ways of doing this. The first is to have existing staff (such as personnel managers) obtain a certificate of competence in occupational testing, having first received familiarisation and other training from test suppliers or other trainers. A second option is to recruit a personnel or other manager who already has the certificate of competence and other appropriate training. The other two options involve being advised by a chartered occupational psychologist working either as a consultant or as an employee. In this chapter, each option is discussed in turn.

Training courses

Reference has already been made to the need to attend a course run by a chartered occupational psychologist if one wishes to use tests. One must start by attending a Level A course which will cover ability and aptitude tests, as well as the basic principles and practice of test administration, scoring and interpretation.

Those wishing to go on to use Level B tests (such as personality questionnaires and interest inventories) will need to attend a further training course geared to the specific tests that they wish to use. Therefore an assessment of the likely worth of specific tests will have to be made before actually attending the training courses. Information about the possible benefits of using the test can be obtained either from the training course organisers and/or from the suppliers of the tests featured in the training courses. Note that courses run by test publishers are usually confined to their own tests, while other trainers often draw on tests from a number of publishers.

It is important that those sent for training have the qualities that will enable them to administer, score and interpret the tests successfully, to obtain suitable facilities and equipment for successful testing, and to defend the appropriate introduction and use of tests. A good level of intelligence is also required to understand the principles involved and explain them to others. Thus, those sent for training must be able to read the test instructions aloud in a clear voice, be able to mark tests quickly and accurately, be able to add up total scores, be able to compare scores with others using norm tables, and be able to explain the results to others both orally and in writing. Finally, competence in the use of personal computers is of increasing value (see Chapter 12). The demands made by Level B training courses are obviously greater than those required for Level A (see Chapter 1).

The cost of training can be considerable. There will certainly be tuition fees and there may well be travelling and residential fees. In addition, there is the cost of absence from work and the cost of obtaining supplies of testing materials.

Once a member of staff is trained, the cost of that person administering a testing programme may be low compared with the other options of regularly involving consultants or employing specialist internal staff, although some test suppliers require registration or licence fees and there is the cost of the test materials too (illustrative costs are given in Chapter 10). However, these short training courses cannot give people the considerable expertise required to develop or evaluate sophisticated testing systems, and an occupational psychologist will be required to do this (see below).

Once an organisation has one or more staff with the full requisite training, it may be sensible to train less senior and expensive staff to do the actual test administration. Training can be given by those holding the BPS certificate (see below) or by attendance on a course for administrators arranged by one of the test suppliers. Details of courses at Levels A and B being run during the following two months appear in the BPS journal *Selection and Development Review*, which appears bi-monthly.

BPS certificates of competence

In the early 1990s, considerable concern was being expressed about the widespread misuse of tests within many organisations. In order to ensure that testing did not fall into general disrepute, The BPS laid down a set of standards in occupational testing, in order to:

- ensure that its members, and other test users, acted in a professional manner, and to agreed minimum standards

- provide a means of recognising users who were competent
- establish minimum standards for training in the use of psychological tests.

The certification scheme that was set up provides an agreed set of standards relating to the fair and effective use of tests, with the need for holders of the certificates to adhere to a code of practice and professional conduct defined by The BPS, and supported by the IPD. The standards have been designed to fulfil a number of functions, including the provision of criteria to be used for assessing competence, and guidance for those who may wish to employ users of tests.

The standards of competence for Level A cover the following areas:

- relevant underpinning knowledge, especially the nature and the theory of testing
- task skills such as test administration and feedback to candidates and clients
- task-management skills relating to, for example, organising procedures and materials
- contingency management skills and dealing with problems, difficulties and breakdowns in routine
- contextual skills relating to the appropriate integration of testing to other parts of the job role, ie when to use tests and when not to
- instrumental skills relating to specific assessment procedures or instruments, eg computer-based procedures.

Some Level A courses run by chartered psychologists are advertised as 'providing training leading to fulfilment of requirements for the BPS certificate of competence in occupational testing at Level A' and so obviously provide automatic qualifications. Other Level A courses 'provide training leading to partial fulfilment of the requirements . . .' and so further verification of testing work is required before the certificate is awarded, subject to acceptable performance.

The BPS currently charges £50 for awarding the certificate, and an annual fee of £15 for joining the register. The BPS encourages test publishers to supply relevant tests only to people who hold the certificate, and employing organisations to use only such staff for testing. Another benefit to members is a free subscription to *Selection and Development*

Review which normally costs £37 per annum. Other services are being developed over time.

The Level B standards apply to those who wish to use tests of habitual or typical performance – personality interests, motivation, values and attitudes – and certificates can be awarded only to those who hold Level A certificates and have demonstrated competence using Level B tests. These standards cover nine units grouped under three broad aspects of competence: foundation knowledge; test use; test choice and evaluation. Through the accumulation of relevant units, people can obtain either an intermediate Level B certificate (competent in the administration and interpretation of one instrument) or a full certificate (competent in two or more). Upgrading is possible, and no further fee is required for Level B membership.

As with Level A, some courses at Level B lead to a Level B intermediate certificate, whereas others require additional work and verification. Readers are advised to contact the test suppliers listed in Appendix 4 or in *Selection and Development Review*, which is distributed free to those with Level A certificates. Full information about the requirements for both Level A and B is available from the BPS (see page xiv for details).

Recruiting certificated staff

It may be appropriate to recruit staff holding a certificate of competence in occupational testing, particularly when the use of tests forms part of the job description for the vacancy to be filled. The BPS holds a register of those holding the certificates and can thus verify any claims made. It may be appropriate to take some account of the particular tests that individual applicants can order without attendance on additional familiarisation courses. More important, it is sensible to find out which Level B tests each applicant is already registered to use, since these tests are still supplied by individual publishers and training in their use can be expensive and time consuming.

Retaining an independent consultant

An independent consultant may be of help in two ways. First, if tests are not already in use, advice can be taken on whether there may be financial or other advantages to be gained through their introduction; in making such a review, account would need to be taken of the sorts of tests that might be used, and whether or not the organisation's own staff should be trained to use them.

Second, if tests are already in use, the consultant's advice may be helpful in determining whether or not the tests are effective and fair, either individually or in combination. In addition, the consultant can advise on the likely benefits of introducing different tests, designing tailor-made tests, etc; the design of tests for specific situations can be an attractive strategy if large numbers are to be tested and/or the qualities to be tested are beyond the normal range of tests. It may also be relevant to review other stages of the recruitment and selection procedure.

Suitable consultant occupational psychologists can best be identified by reference to the Register of Chartered Occupational Psychologists published by The British Psychological Society (see Appendix 1) and by reference to the Society's register of those holding the certificate of competence in occupational testing. Alternatively, refer to a directory published by the BPS called *The Directory of Chartered Psychologists* (price £36). The directory was put together specifically as a source of independent advisers/consultants to guide the uninitiated through the plethora of tests available in the market-place. Psychologists who have an interest either in the sales of particular tests or in running training courses in testing should obviously disclose their interest in preliminary discussions.

Advice on testing is sometimes offered by consultants and others who are not psychologists. But it is only The British Psychological Society that has drawn up standards about the use of tests, and only the Division of Occupational Psychology that has a code of conduct geared to industrial and commercial practice.

Employing specialist staff

The fourth possibility is for an organisation to consider the appointment of its own occupational psychologist. This again should ensure an impartial assessment of the potential benefits of testing and other assessment methods. However, the commitment to employ an occupational psychologist on anything other than a short-term contract will be making assumptions about the value of using tests and about the level of recruitment in the months and years ahead. While the psychologist might be able to contribute to many other aspects of the organisation besides selection, the short-term and long-term role of the psychologist would need to be fully considered before this option was chosen. This strategy is most appropriate when there is scope for large-scale testing and assessment and when considerable savings can be made by developing in-house tests and training courses tailor-made to the organisation's needs. Major UK organisations employing their own occupational psychologists include the Civil Service, British Telecom, The Post Office and British Airways.

All in all, there may be advantages in seeking advice from an independent occupational psychologist initially, and then evaluating the other options in the light of the benefits that testing and the other skills of occupational psychologists are likely to bring (see Appendix 2).

Tests from other sources

Because of the cost of obtaining reputable psychological tests, some managers may be tempted to try some of the material available from non-psychologists which are claimed to measure ability, personality etc. Although such materials are often well presented, there is seldom any technical information of the kind described in Chapter 2 to back up claims about the value of the techniques. For example, in June 1986 the *Guidance and Assessment Review* (now called *Selection and Development Review*, and published by The BPS) carried a report of the systematic analysis of two inventories of this kind and concluded that there was little evidence to suggest that either could justify the apparently detailed analysis of personality which the authors claimed for their system of profile analysis.

If these or other instruments are used there is not only the danger that they may select the wrong people, but that their use could not be justified at an industrial tribunal and that the reputation of the employing organisation could be severely damaged; mention has already been made of the fact that some tests that fail to meet psychometric standards have appealing graphic design, and those contemplating the use of tests must be careful not to base their judgements on appearances alone.

There are two other reasons why some unproven tests may be widely used. The first is that some managers lack the kind of information available in this book and do not appreciate the kind of information that should be available about a test.

The second reason is the widespread use of a 'ploy' to sell supposed measures of personality; the ploy involves asking managers to complete a questionnaire and subsequently discussing their results with them. The results can seem quite impressive, a powerful and personal demonstration of validity. Unfortunately, it is no such thing.

This was nicely demonstrated in a well-known study by Stagner (1958) who gave a personality inventory to a group of 68 personnel managers at a conference, then took their papers away for scoring. Later, the participants were given a report describing their personality as shown by their results. Fifty per cent rated their report as 'amazingly accurate', 40 per cent as 'rather good', and the remaining 10 per cent judged it as 'about half and half'; none rated their reports as 'more wrong than right' or as 'almost entirely wrong'. It was then revealed to the managers involved that they had in fact all been given exactly the same personality description, which was nothing to do with the personality inventory. How could the participants have been so convinced yet so deceived? Nor are they alone. This study has been repeated many times and the same results found, even when the participants have been given reports containing unflattering descriptions of themselves.

This phenomenon is called 'the Barnum effect' after the showman of that name. It is in effect a trick. The personality descriptions are loaded with vague generalities which are actually applicable to most people; statements like, 'I am sometimes not as confident as I appear'. Not surprisingly, when faced with a whole series of such truisms presented by a consultant or other 'expert' as being the product of a carefully constructed test, people tend to be impressed. After all, what they are being given is for the most part correct as far as it goes; the trouble is, it does not differentiate one person from another and cannot be of any use in decision making.

Something similar happens when you visit a fortune teller ('I see a tall, dark stranger') or when graphologists 'prove' that handwriting analysis is the key to personality assessment by giving a description based on somebody's signature. Although it often goes against the grain to admit it, judging the worth of a personality measure on the basis of one's perceptions of its accuracy in describing oneself is woefully inadequate.

Tests developed outside the UK

Test materials developed in the USA and other overseas countries sometimes have good technical information but can require substantial adaptation before they can be used with confidence in the UK. The services of occupational psychologists should be retained to make this adaptation.

Summary

Essentially there are four ways in which organisations can obtain and use reputable psychological tests:

- by their personnel or other staff obtaining The British Psychological Society's certificates in occupational testing (Levels A and/or B)
- by recruiting staff with the certificates in occupational testing
- by retaining an occupational psychologist as an external consultant
- by employing an occupational psychologist or team of psychologists.

Any tests obtained by other means are unlikely to be effective, particularly as they will be administered, scored and interpreted by inadquately trained or completely untrained staff. Beware of 'the Barnum effect'. Remember too that tests that have been professionally developed overseas may require substantial work before being suitable for use in the UK.

5
Strategies for using tests in selection

This chapter is about planning how tests are to be used. If testing is to feature in a number of procedures within the same organisation, testing strategy needs to be thought through because:

- While the same tests can be used for a variety of different applications or purposes eg selection, development, individual counselling, team building etc, it is normal to limit the use of individual tests or questionnaires to particular situations. If this were not done, some people in an organisation might be given a reasoning test to help them to formulate a personal development plan, and then might be asked to take the same test a few days later as a part of an assessment for promotion; re-taking a test in this way is likely to favour the individuals concerned and to give them an unfair advantage over any other applicants

- It could be time-consuming and expensive for personnel and other staff to become qualified to use a different test for every possible situation.

Strategies may concern:

- the purpose of testing, eg
  (a) as part of a selection procedure
  (b) for development or other purposes
- how the tests will be administered
- whether internal and external applicants can be treated in the same way.

Testing as part of a selection procedure

Tests can be given:

(i) as an aid to shortlisting

(ii) as part of the main selection procedure

(iii) as part of a detailed check on the final few.

Tests as an aid to shortlisting

Imagine a situation in which reasoning tests are being used as part of a time-consuming selection procedure in which a large proportion of the applicants are failing to reach the minimum standards required on the tests. If there is good reason to believe that performance on these tests will be a valid predictor of subsequent job performance and that they will not discriminate unfairly (two key criteria for choosing tests for use at any stage of a selection procedure) there may be considerable savings in time and effort by using the tests at an earlier stage in the selection process as a method of sifting. For example, the first stage in a revised approach to selection might be for applicants to complete an application form; the second stage might comprise a systematic sift of the forms combined with a short telephone interview with the more promising candidates; the third stage might entail calling a group of the more promising candidates in (a) to give them information about the organisation and the particular vacancies (b) to administer tests and (c) to give brief interviews concerning key issues or requirements. As a result of this preliminary work, the success rate among those invited back to the time-consuming selection procedure is likely to rise to an acceptable level.

It may be possible to make even bigger savings by 'streamlining' the testing arrangements; for example, applicants might be brought to a central point to be tested in large groups by means of pencil-and-paper tests and in this way the cost of the administrator's time could be minimised. Under normal circumstances a single administrator can test about 20 people (for larger groups assistance is required) and advantage can sometimes be taken of low-cost rail and coach fares. Further savings can be made by using special answer sheets that can be scored quickly or even fed into a computer for scoring. A few major employers dealing with very large numbers may find it worthwhile to have tests administered on small business computers or computer terminals so that scoring can then take place automatically (see Chapter 12).

Sifting procedures of this kind are in fact operated by major employers receiving large numbers of applications. Each year large organisations such as the Post Office receive several thousand applications from graduates seeking a career in management, and the decision as to which applicant to call to the main selection procedures (which may be an assessment centre lasting 24 hours) is partly based on the result of job-related tests. A more radical sift has been carried out by the Civil Service Commission who have been faced with up to 10,000 applicants for as few as 200 vacancies for administration trainees; tests are used to reduce the number of candidates by 80 per cent or more, but some would regard this high level of dependence on tests as contentious.

However, four points need to be made about the use of tests as a means of shortlisting. The first is that when tests are used as a way of reducing large numbers there is often a temptation to control the number of applicants invited to the final selection by the simple method of raising or lowering the 'cut-off' or 'pass' mark without thinking through all the possible consequences. There are real dangers in this kind of *ad hoc* approach – if those with low marks are 'passed' they may be found to lack the abilities required to do the job, while restriction to those with only the highest marks may eliminate candidates with other strengths. This issue is discussed in more detail in Chapter 8.

Second, tests are not the only method of shortlisting. Others include shortlisting on the basis of replies on standard or supplementary application forms and some organisations are now using 'bio-data', an approach in which numerical values are assigned to candidates' biographical replies according to research based on past applicants. For internal candidates, supervisors' reports can be another factor to take into account.

A third point about shortlisting is that there is sometimes scope for reducing numbers by giving more opportunity for self-selection; in this way, the cost of testing and interviewing people who eventually decide they do not want the job can be avoided. So, while it is the normal aim of an advertisement to attract as many applicants as possible, an advertisement for a job which is likely to be popular might also contain information about some of the less appealing aspects of the work; for example, the need to spend a lot of time away from home, or to be on call to deal with emergencies, or to work in difficult or unpleasant conditions.

When organising and running selection procedures it is possible to calculate, or at least estimate, the ratios between the numbers attending the final selection procedure, the numbers offered appointments, the numbers accepting and the numbers actually starting. Shortlisting or self-selection requires an excess of applicants over the numbers that need to be called to the subsequent stages in the selection procedure. If there is no such excess there is a conflict between the use of shortlisting methods and filling all the vacancies. Under these circumstances there is a range of possible management strategies ranging from re-advertising to reviewing and adjusting the nature of the work and the working conditions (see also Chapter 7).

Tests as part of the main selection procedure

There are several reasons why it could be desirable for tests to form part of the main selection procedure rather than be a separate part. First, separate testing may be considered unacceptable by candidates; this might be true if considerable travel was to be involved so that applicants might require a day's absence to attend testing and a further day to attend for interview.

A second reason for testing as part of the final procedure is that stock can then be taken of both the strengths and weaknesses of each candidate. However, if this is done some difficult decisions may have to be faced – for example, a candidate with a number of past achievements may have a single indifferent test score and his or her potential for work at a higher level may therefore be questioned. Since test scores can sometimes be very good guides to potential it can be difficult to make the 'right' decision. Clearly a decision based on evidence from follow-up studies of past selections would be preferable to an *ad hoc* decision (see Chapter 10).

A third reason for testing being part of the final selection procedure could be to allow all internal candidates the opportunity to take part in the full assessment and thus to confirm an organisation's interest in the development of its own staff whenever possible.

Tests as part of a detailed check on the 'final few'

Some organisations use tests as part of a final check on applicants rather than in a preliminary sift. There can be several reasons for this, including the fact that the final assessors may be senior staff from a head office or other location who have access to tests which are not available locally.

Sometimes consultant occupational psychologists (from within or outside the organisation) are asked to advise at this late stage of selection and to use tests as part of their procedures. This strategy is of particular use when those involved in the earlier stages of selection are not accredited test users, when the most appropriate tests are available only to the psychologists, and/or when a view is required of how applicants compare with standards outside a particular organisation. The individual assessment of candidates may also be preferred when there is a need for security about the vacancies and/or the individual applicants.

A final reason for delaying the involvement of experts until the end of the procedure is the view that their in-depth and sometimes expensive assessments should be confined to the most promising candidates only. (See Chapter 9.)

Testing for development and other purposes

Tests can be used not only for selection but also as an aid to helping employees with their career development. Tests can be used to help gauge suitability for specific vacancies or training opportunities (such as computer programming), or can be used as part of a process of helping individuals plan their career development by providing them with objective feedback about their abilities and aptitudes, personality values and interests.

There are two main ways in which tests can be used as an aid to career development. First, they can be used by an occupational psychologist or trained personnel manager working with just one individual; the individual being counselled may agree to take a variety of tests and questionnaires and may then be counselled about the results and the implications. Such work is demanding of the individual counsellor, who needs to have a wide breadth and depth of knowledge both about tests and occupational information both within and outside the organisation. However, such counselling can be carried out in confidence and at relatively short notice.

A second approach to career development which may involve tests is the assessment centre (see Chapter 11). Initially, such centres were another form of selection, attempting to assess those individuals who had the attributes identified as being important in long-term managerial success (Dulewicz 1991). In time, however, the emphasis has changed and many assessment centres are now much more oriented to helping individuals to achieve greater awareness of their own strengths and weaknesses and subsequently making use of this information in planning their development. Assessment centres are administratively more complex and are therefore difficult to arrange at short notice. Participants are often required to work together and/or compete against each other, so that they often have the opportunity to assess their own performance against that of the other participants. Because assessment centres often involve several specially trained personnel and other managers with contrasting backgrounds and experience, there can be a wide and informed view of opportunities within the organisation.

Psychological tests may be used as part of the assessment centre programme in this context just as in the selection setting. Indeed, it is not unknown for them also to be used as a way of selecting people to go on to assessment centres. This reflects the fact that assessment centres are expensive and that not everyone can benefit from attending, so it makes sense for both individuals and organisations to try to ensure that only those who will get something from the experience go through it. Further, sifting can help to prevent people attending the centres who would find the procedures excessively demanding. So here, the use of tests in selection and in development come together.

Psychometric measures are given as an aid to self-development in many other settings as well; typically, they are administered to managers on training courses so that they can see the results and have an opportunity to discuss the implications for their personal approach to work. Personality measures such as the Myers-Briggs Type Indicator®, OPQ® and Cattell 16PF are all frequently used in this way.

Finally, tests have been used as an aid to the development of teams as well as individuals. Belbin (1981) and others have shown how work groups, put together on the basis of the right mix of personality characteristics, can perform more effectively than randomly constituted groups, even when the latter are intellectually more able. So, for example, the ideal management team would not only have the appropriate skills in specialist terms (eg finance, operations, personnel, sales and marketing) but would also complement each other in the way that they would work together at a particular problem.

Test administration

Testing procedures have become increasingly streamlined. Originally, many tests were administered individually, but in their place pencil-and-paper tests were used on a group basis because of the ease of administration. The latest development is that not only are some tests both administered and scored by computer, but also that the test items administered to individual candidates can be altered according to their speed of response and correctness of reply.

The capital outlay involved on computerised testing is considerable, but it does have attractions for major organisations handling large numbers of applicants each year (see Chapter 12).

Testing internal and external applicants

There may be two arguments for adopting different policies towards internal and external candidates in terms of the tests to be taken and the scores to be considered acceptable. The first argument can arise when internal candidates already have experience bearing on the job for which they are applying, so that the amount of learning and adjustment they will need to make may appear to be small and it can be argued that assessments of performance on the related jobs may be a good guide to performance in the new job. By contrast, the demand on external candidates new to the organisation may appear to be high. Accordingly, it might be proposed that testing should be carried out only on the external applicants. Alternatively, some differences may be allowed in the levels of test scores considered acceptable for each group. In deciding, much will depend on the ease or difficulty with which the transition has been made by past internal candidates and the confidence that can be placed in the assessments of performance. Account should also be taken of the likelihood of job experience affecting test scores. In particular, care should be taken that the procedure does not 'pass' internal candidates who lack the potential to develop further.

A second argument for treating each group differently is that there is a stronger case for providing internal candidates with 'feedback' as to how they got on in the selection procedure since it is important to sustain the motivation of employees who have been rejected. No doubt many external candidates would also like such feedback, particularly when they have taken a substantive test battery lasting several hours or even a day; they should be given it whenever possible (see Chapter 8).

Summary

Test users often have a number of decisions to make about exactly how to make use of tests. The decisions include:

- whether, and at what stage, tests should be used for selection

- whether, and at what stage, tests should be used for development

- how tests should be administered and scored

- whether internal and external candidates should be treated in the same way.

This chapter has addressed the pros and cons of various options. However, tests can be used in many different ways (Tyler and Miller 1986) and the final decision must be made according to specific circumstances.

6
Introducing tests for selection
(I) Choosing the tests

This chapter considers how potential users should choose tests. While, for simplicity, it concentrates on the use of tests for selection, it should be borne in mind that:

- tests can be used as part of procedures for other purposes (eg career development, team building);

- tests can be used to help assess a very wide range of people and types and levels of work, ranging from manufacturing to sales work and from trainees to managing directors.

Essential preliminaries

Before choosing tests it is important to have a clear idea of the range of qualities or characteristics required for successful job performance. This in turn depends on an appreciation of the work to be done. Details of the work to be done are normally collected together as a job description, while the qualities or characteristics required for successful job performance form a person-specification. Selection methods, including tests, than have to be chosen. Each stage is discussed in turn.

Job descriptions

The main purpose of a job description for selection purposes is to identify the tasks and activities which are crucial to the successful job performance. From these details the qualities required in ideal applicants (the person-specification) can be assessed by a deductive process. In addition, the job description should provide information about features of the work likely to attract (or even deter) candidates, including hours of work, pay, etc. Such information can be circulated so that a degree of self-selection can occur.

It is rare to find comprehensive and up-to-date job descriptions waiting to be used for selection purposes and more often than not information has to be specially collected; this is traditionally done using a check-list to cover salient features, such as the aims and objectives of the job, responsibilities, resources available and so on; it is normal, too, to involve current job holders, their bosses, etc, so as to build up a detailed picture.

In practice, the amount of detail to be collected will depend on the number of vacancies to be filled and the importance and complexity of the job. If the vacancy is important there are a number of special techniques that can be used to make sure that a comprehensive picture is obtained; examples of the main types of techniques, which can be used singly or in combination, are as follows:

- *Interview:* staff may use a structured process such as Flanagan's critical incident technique, Kelly's repertory grid technique, or perhaps internally-developed structured questionnaires which have particular relevance to the type of work being done.

- *Job analysis questionnaires:* these have been developed as a result of extensive research and continuous modifications. Examples are McCormick's position analysis questionnaire for lower-level jobs, and an equivalent version for supervisory and management jobs; some are now computer-administered, with results being analysed and printed by expert systems.

- *Diary technique:* this involves the incumbent keeping a diary of his key activities over a long period.

The person specification

As described earlier, the person-specification comprises a list of qualities to be sought in an ideal applicant; it is based on inferences made from the job description about the personal qualities required.

Again a check-list approach can have an advantage in terms of helping to make sure that nothing important is missed. The most widely used framework in the UK is the late Professor Alec Rodger's seven point plan (1953), which recommends specifying the characteristics required in the ideal applicant under seven headings:

1   Physical make-up

2   Attainments

3   General intelligence

4   Special aptitudes

5   Interests

6   Disposition (personality)

7   Circumstances (domestic, mobility, family traditions, etc).[1]

From the information collected in the job description, the person-spec-ification is deduced for each of the seven headings. For some jobs there may be requirements in terms of height and weight; entry requirements to the police service are often cited as an example. However, it should be noted that any arbitrary requirements may be challenged on the grounds of unfair discrimination – in the USA, for example, the height requirement for police officers is now based on the argument that they should be tall enough to aim a gun over the roof of a car while using the car as protection. Minimum requirements should be realistic and should relate to the demands of the job and behaviour required for successful performance.

In drawing up lists of this kind it is good practice to distinguish between essential and desirable characteristics; it is important not to have too many essentials or it may be impossible to find anyone who meets the specifications. Should this happen, matters will have to be resolved by, for example, relaxing some of the essential criteria, reviewing the pay or other benefits or even changing the way that the work is to be done (see also Chapter 8).

When drawing up the person-specification it can sometimes be help-ful to identify any contra-indicators, that is features that may make some applicants unsuitable; for example, regular commitments in the local community would be a contra-indicator for a job involving frequent travel away from home, unless of course the applicant was prepared to change his or her lifestyle. However, in practice what matters is that the applicant is able to take on frequent travel away from home, and not any other details of the candidate's life-style.

When using check-lists, such as the seven point plan, it is normal to specify at least one characteristic under each heading. However, there will of course be differences in the types of quality sought according to the nature of the vacancy to be filled. For example, in the selection of a senior manager, some of the skills, abilities and personality characteris-tics in the following list might be considered important:

1   In the light of subsequent equal opportunities legislation any questions should be confined to exploring job-related issues such as availability and mobility rather than circumstances *per se*.

- oral communication skills
- written communication skills
- emotional adjustment
- analytical ability
- fertility of mind
- flexibility
- drive
- ascendancy
- planning and organisation
- social skill
- delegation and control.

Choosing the selection method

The next stage of the selection process is to choose the appropriate selection methods to assess the qualities considered to be important. Possibilities include:

- application forms
- references and other written reports
- interviews (individual or panel)
- psychometric tests
- psychometric questionnaires
- group discussions, simulation exercises, etc. in which candidates work together or compete with each other.

In addition, self-selection among applicants is encouraged by many organisations (see Chapter 5).

A useful aid to choosing the appropriate methods is a matrix with the methods down one side, and the requirements (eg the headings from the seven point plan) across the top. A tick is then placed in the appropriate cell of the matrix for each method that provides relevant information for each heading, ensuring that each heading is covered by at least one method. It is preferable that more than one method provides information about each requirement so that there is a cross check. Any inconsistencies can be investigated through the interview by careful scrutiny of the written data or by following up references if possible.

Tests and questionnaires are particularly valuable for assessing intelligence and special aptitudes under the seven point plan framework, and for providing structured, quasi-objective data about interests and disposition. Apart from assessment centres (which often involve tests and questionnaires) the other methods have shown very poor reliability and validity for assessing these characteristics. In contrast, tests and questionnaires also have some limitations as when, for example, collecting data on availability for work or physical make-up.

Which test?

As noted in Chapter 1, there are over 5,000 psychometric instruments available in the English language alone. Even restricting choice to those available to non-psychologists, potential test users face a psychometric jungle, a jungle with more than its fair share of predators! The route might be charted by three As: (a) availability (b) appropriateness (c) acceptability.

(a) Availability

One obvious constraint on choice is the availability of tests, either in terms of the organisation having staff qualified to use them or in terms of their being obtainable by non-psychologists at all (see Chapter 1). However, all the tests described in Chapter 2 (and many others) are potentially available providing that people have been sent on the appropriate courses.

The restriction of supply to trained staff does mean that an organisation considering using tests needs first to audit its own resources of staff who are trained in this area. Some staff may have been trained while working for other employers. Should there be few or none, then a decision has to be made on whether to invest in sending people on the relevant courses or to have a special course run for the organisation (both of which may mean a certain amount of delay) or to bring in consultant occupational psychologists (see Chapter 4).

(b) Appropriateness

Imagine that a person-specification has been drawn up listing, amongst other things, emotional stability and extraversion as desirable attributes for the person appointed. As the tests must be appropriate to assess these characteristics, the next stage is to survey what is available. It may turn out that there is a whole string of instruments purporting to measure these qualities of emotional stability and extraversion. How then can a decision be made as to which of them is best and most appropriate? Factors to consider include the following:

- evidence of reliability

- evidence of validity

- evidence of the use of the test elsewhere

- normative data

- preventing unfair discrimination.

Evidence of reliability: The reliability of a test is a measure of its consistency (see Chapter 2). Any worthwhile test should be supported by evidence of this. It will normally be summarised in terms of a single figure ranging from 0 to +1, with 0 indicating a complete lack of reliability and +1 showing perfect reliability; if the figures were based on test-retest reliability, +1 would mean people were getting exactly the same absolute or relative test scores on separate occasions (see Chapter 2). Perfect reliability is never achieved, but in ability tests reliability of +0.75 or above based on a sample size of at least 100, should be expected.

Measures of personality are subject to rather greater variation, which is understandable as the expression of personality is perhaps more susceptible to transient influence than is the demonstration of ability when individuals are doing their best to perform well on tests. For personality measures, a reliability of +0.65 or above based on a sample size of 100 may be considered acceptable.

Evidence of validity: Validity measurements are evidence about whether the test is measuring what it purports to measure and different kinds of validity were outlined in Chapter 2. The measurement can be illustrated by the extent to which a test has demonstrated that it relates to some external criterion as, for example, tests given to bank clerks might relate to their subsequent job performance. Again, as in the case of reliability, the evidence is likely to be summarised in the form of a validity co-efficient that ranges from −1 to +1. A correlation of +1 means that on a graph plotting test score against job performance for a number of individuals there would be a linear relationship between test scores and performance so that the person with the highest test score has the highest job performance. This is illustrated in Figure 1.

Figure 1

A graph showing a correlation of +1 between test scores and job performance. Each cross represents the test score/job performance for one individual; for simplicity only five individuals are represented.

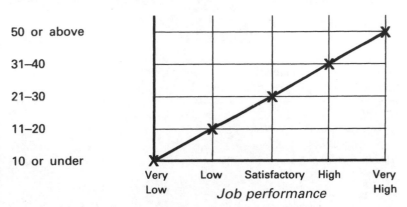

A correlation of –1 would mean that the person with the lowest test score had the highest performance. A correlation of 0 would mean that there is no relationship between the scores and job performance.

Test manuals should contain data about validity. For example, the manual for a numerical reasoning test might show that for a sample of people selected for the job of bank clerk the test scores correlated +0.35 with the ratings of performance made on those same people by their supervisors one year later; this would mean that there was a tendency for those scoring well on the test to perform well, but prediction would be far from certain.

The size of validity correlations quoted in manuals may at first sight seem low but there are plenty of reasons, some of which are dealt with below, why it is unrealistic to expect high ones. For various technical reasons it is difficult to specify precisely what is and is not acceptable in terms of validity co-efficients; under some circumstances, validities as low as +0.10 might make worthwhile improvements to the effectiveness of selection although correlations of +0.50 might be an initial target and +0.20 a realistic goal. Remember too that results from tests are often used in combination because successful job applicants need to be competent in several different ways. For example, an applicant for a clerical job might need to be competent at numerical calculations, understanding the meaning of words, filing, and carrying out simple

79

instructions using tables of information; the four relevant tests might individually have rather low predictive power but together might reach an altogether more useful level.

Whenever looking at validity information in test manuals, check the size of the samples involved in the validity study as well as the correlation itself (see below).

Table 1

Test Score	Number of promotions gained in first four years			
	0 (%)	1 (%)	2 (%)	
51–60	60	30	10	(100%)
61–70	40	35	25	(100%)
71+	25	35	40	(100%)

People who find it difficult to understand the implications of validity may find the hypothetical example in Table 1 helpful. Imagine that a test has been given to help select for a job. The test results are being validated by comparing the test scores with the number of promotions of each individual during the first four years. The table shows the percentage of people who achieved 0, 1 or 2 promotions during that period.

In the example, 40 per cent of the candidates who obtain a test score of 71 or above go on to achieve two promotions in the next four years, compared with just 10 per cent of those who had test scores in the 51–60 range; increases in test scores seem to be clearly predictive of career success over the period examined. However, given just one test score, it can be seen that the Table is by no means a perfect guide to the probable success of the individual with that score.

Validity evidence often has two components, the test score and the measure of performance (or criterion measurement). A wide range of criterion measures may be utilised, ranging from specific measures of task performance to rather broader indicators of success such as performance appraisal ratings, salary increases and promotions. None of these criteria are themselves perfect measures of performance. The promotion system in the organisation will not be 100 per cent accurate in identifying those most deserving of advancement, partly because in many cases the appraisal process to which it is linked is subject to all sorts of biases and imperfections. Thus, using either promotions gained or appraisal ratings as the criteria by which the effectiveness of tests is judged is never going to yield a wholly accurate assessment of how good a test actually is.

Even when objective measures of performance are available, as in the case of many sales jobs, they seldom tell the whole story; the sales made have to be interpreted against the background of the potential of the territory, the competition, the manner in which the results were achieved (have claims or promises been made that will prove difficult to live up to and hence make selling in that area more difficult next year?), and so on. But whatever their deficiencies, criteria of the kinds mentioned here are the best that are usually available and are certainly far, far better than no validation evidence at all.

In response to demands from potential test users for better information about test validity, test designers and publishers are starting to respond in two ways. The first approach is to offer computer print-outs detailing large numbers of correlations between tests and performance criteria. Some of these correlations will be high and will be offered as evidence of the worth of the test or tests.

However, as indicated in the Preface, such information should not be accepted as proof. When a number of correlations are calculated, some large correlations will arise as random departures from zero underlying conditions – in other words, they will have occurred by chance. Correlations are not explanations – remember that tomatoes are eaten by 98 per cent of juvenile delinquents!

In Appendix 6 we suggest that test users and others making decisions about tests should look for evidence of worth over and above the size of correlation. Four kinds of evidence might be considered: (i) that *specific* hypotheses have been made and tested; (ii) that an appropriate level of statistical significance has been used; (iii) that there are theoretical or practical explanations for any large correlations that are found; and (iv) that similar findings have been found in independent studies.

The other way in which statistical data about test validity may be offered is in the form of a meta-analysis – that is, the results from a series of validity studies are combined in order to assess the overall worth of the test. The technique is respectable in theory, but in practice caution should be exercised before accepting the findings. Appendix 7 describes meta-analysis, and the associated issue of validity generalisation, in more detail.

Occasionally, test users may be faced with several alternative tests each with similar availability, reliability and validity. How then may a choice be made?

Under such circumstances, a decision may rest on the precise reason for requiring the tests. For example, if the primary purpose for testing is to assess suitability for a particular job, the ideal kind of validity evidence to be sought from the manuals of the test under consideration will be that they have shown an acceptable level of correlation with some form of performance rating or other measures in identical work. However, beware of deciding that work is 'identical' simply because a common job title is used (see Chapter 1) and be prepared to take professional advice since differences may affect the worth of the tests significantly.

Where the aim of testing is wider, and the concern is to predict performance over a number of jobs that an individual might do in the first couple of years, and possibly to give some indication of career potential, the prospective test user should seek evidence of correlations with performance measures over a period of time and with indices of progress (salary growth, number of promotions etc).

The question, then, is whether the test has been shown to predict the outcome required. That said, however, the imperfections of each of the various performance criteria used are such that the more validation evidence there is, preferably including a range of criterion measures, the better.

Evidence of the use of the test elsewhere: Although it is important to know whether proper validation studies have been carried out, such studies are rare because of the sample sizes needed and the time and experience required. But while there may not be a wealth of validity data, the tests may be widely used and there may be considerable information about their use and acceptability which could influence a decision about whether or not to use the tests in particular circumstances.

Enquiries to the test publishers, to consultant occupational psychologists and to experienced users, and reference to books and other publications describing test usage (eg Miller, 1975), can therefore be useful. Some of the information may be positive – for example, major companies may comment favourably about the worth of the tests, about the ease of administration and scoring and so on. Conversely, the information may be negative – for example, applicants elsewhere may be failing to understand instructions, test booklets may be found to have pages missing or to be poorly printed, and so on.

Finding that a test or series of tests have been adopted widely means that if they are given in the selection context, there is always the chance that candidates will have encountered them before. Indeed, since people tend to apply for more than one job at the same time, it is not at all uncommon to find candidates taking some of the same tests for different organisations in selection procedures just a few days apart. This inevitably carries the danger of familiarity breeding enhanced performance; for example, on the second and third presentations of an ability test candidates are likely to get marginally higher scores, but may not improve further thereafter; however, exceptions have been noticed and test manuals should ideally give information on this point. In those instances where the individual has also been provided with feedback on the results of a previous assessment, this may considerably affect the attitude to encountering the same tests again; personality measures may be particularly subject to distortion where the person feels the need to try to modify the picture that emerged last time.

Very widespread use of a test does carry with it this problem, and ideally test publishers should provide information on the effects of previous testing both with and without feedback of results. Alternatively, users might aim to compile their own information. But at present if equally good but less frequently used measures are available it may be worth opting for them. Either way, it is good practice to check whether candidates have been through any similar procedures recently – and if they have, what tests were involved (they may not know the names, but the descriptions given will often give a good clue as to the identity). This sometimes allows users either to change the tests to be given or at least to be aware of some possible effect of prior experience. Unless the previous testing session was very recent – in the last week or two – it is unlikely that scores on ability tests will be affected significantly.

Normative design: The use of a test elsewhere does, however, have advantages. It is of little value to know that someone has achieved a score of 56 on a test, where the possible range of scores is 10 to 75, without knowing how others compare with this individual's score on the test. In other words, normative data are required (see Chapter 1). An important factor in choosing tests is whether or not they can provide normative data relevant to particular needs. For example, an organisation selecting school-leavers for clerical jobs may want tests of numerical calculation and verbal ability that have normative data for 16-year-olds who have been entered for the highest GCSE grades; there would be little point in judging the school-leavers' scores by comparing them with the performance of graduates on the same tests.

Problems of some complexity can arise because abilities can influence career decisions and people tend to stop studying subjects in which they are making little progress. Imagine an engineering company assessing candidates for jobs in technical sales. Direct comparisons of candidates with an engineering or technical background with those of people who had a predominantly arts background might not aid a sound decision since as a group the latter would probably do significantly better on verbal and significantly worse on numerical or spatial ability measures than would the engineers. Over and above the test scores judgements would need to be made about the speed with which non-technical people might pick up technical knowledge, and the extent to which technical people might develop verbal sales skills. The availability of suitable training might be a key factor.

As far as possible, choose tests with norms that allow the comparison of like with like; the norms should also be based on samples that are large enough to give confidence that they are representative (at least 100 and preferably 200 or more). The manual that accompanies the test should contain that information. While it is possible, and desirable, for an organisation eventually to build up its own norms, this clearly takes some time.

Unfair discrimination: Another important standard by which to assess the suitability of any test is whether its use is consistent with equal opportunities legislation (see Chapter 3).

(c) Acceptability

Having run through some of the main aspects of judging the appropriateness of tests, it is time to consider the final element in the choice of process. This concerns the acceptability of the measures adopted to those being assessed. Factors to be considered include (i) the presentation of the test material (ii) the face validity of the tests and (iii) the acceptability of the test items.

The general presentation of the test items: Poorly produced, dog-eared or drab test booklets do not endear themselves to candidates nor inspire confidence among clients or other managers. Appearance should therefore be a factor in choice.

More important, however, is the apparent nature of the tests themselves. What are the people being tested likely to think the tests are for? How will they feel about what they are being asked to do or say?

Face validity: This refers to the extent to which a test looks as though it is measuring what it sets out to measure (see Chapter 1). Whether it looks the part or not is actually a very unreliable guide to the real, criterion-related validity of a test. But face validity does matter in other ways. With ability tests, there is little problem, since the type of intellectual ability being assessed is usually fairly obvious and knowing it will make scant difference to anyone's performance. Also, the rationale for giving ability tests is perhaps more readily (but by no means universally) accepted by candidates than is the rationale for personality measures. It is here that most of the trouble arises.

Developing personality questionnaires that have high face validity reduces the danger of alienating the individual being assessed. Such alienation might well have happened when applicants for normal managerial posts were asked to complete a personality inventory, much used in the USA, which included questions about bowel movements. Applicants might reasonably have wondered what on earth this was supposed to be assessing and what relevance it had to the job in question; they might become increasingly annoyed at such an intrusive and seemingly irrelevant line of questioning, to the extent that a gut feeling of quite another kind would be telling them that this is not the kind of organisation in which they wish to work.

There are of course two problems here. One is the obscure purpose of the exercise and the other is the unacceptable nature of particular questionnaire items. Unfortunately, they interact with each other to produce a potentially unfavourable response. It is possible to construct personality inventories that are much more transparent and which thus are more likely to have higher face validity. People can see what is being measured and can relate it to the purpose of the assessment. In addition, such readily understandable measures are easier to use in any subsequent feedback session. Unfortunately, it also means that the candidates are in a better position to try to manipulate the impression they give of themselves on such measures; it potentially helps them to fake.

Turning to the problem of personality inventory items that may seem bizarre or extreme in some way, these are usually present as elements in scales that tap aspects of emotional adjustment, or maladjustment to be more accurate. Or they may have the purpose of picking up people who are at the outer limits of some personality dimension (which again may have implications about the individual's adjustment in a more restricted sense). If personality measures are employed which avoid the use of such items, then it will probably be at the cost of not assessing these aspects of the person as well as they might have done. Incidentally, it should be pointed out here that some people do endorse extreme items of this kind; they do not always see them as being odd and do not cover-up (though equally obviously, some do!).

Opinion is divided about the best way forward, some taking the view that the candidate's self-knowledge is helpful, others distrusting it because they fear that some candidates will manipulate their replies. Accordingly many procedures seek both to assess candidates and to give them the opportunity to report assessments of themselves; some go further and also ask the candidates to assess each other.

If a choice is to be made it should reflect particular circumstances. If it is of particular concern that those selected be emotionally resilient, because the jobs concerned are high-stress, then the balance may be felt to tip in favour of using measures that may be a little lower in acceptability to the candidate. In other circumstances, as when there is strong competition to recruit the best candidates, it might be felt that while there is still a need to assess them, it should not be done in such a fashion that it drives them into the arms of the competitors.

Acceptability: consider how tests will appear to candidates. For example, when choosing personality measures, the sensible thing to do is to go through the inventories and reflect on how they will seem to the candidates. Even if it is felt to be essential to use questionnaires that ask some of the more extreme types of question, there is still a great deal that can be done to minimise any adverse reactions; this is discussed later in this book (administration of tests and feedback of results).

Finally, under the heading of acceptability, the use of microcomputers in testing needs to be considered. This is discussed in detail in Chapter 12.

Summary

Whether or not to choose tests should be based on the following:

- the nature of the work to be done
- an analysis of the characteristics of ideal applicants
- a review of other possible selection methods.

If tests are to be used, choice should be based on:

- availability

- appropriateness, including
  reliability
  validity
  the use of the test elsewhere
  normative data
  avoiding unfair discrimination

- acceptability, including
  face validity
  the acceptability of individual items.

A case study, describing the choice of tests for the selection of clerical staff, appears as Appendix 1.

7
Introducing tests for selection
(II) Planning and implementation

This chapter deals with four issues: getting agreement to proceed with testing; organising testing; maintaining a large-scale testing programme; and testing individuals.

Getting agreement to proceed with testing

Assume that a stage has been reached where a strong case can be made for the use of tests as part of a procedure for the selection of graduate entrants (broadly similar principles would apply if other groups were to be involved). The recommendation to use tests could be based on a number of points, including the following:

- A follow-up of some recent graduate entrants in your organisation has shown that some have given up because of pressure of work while others have been given poor reports at the end of induction training and at the end of their first year of employment.

- An analysis of the work done by graduate entrants has been carried out and the qualities and skills required for successful job performance has been identified; from these analyses possible tests have been identified.

- The manuals for the tests show 'good' evidence of the worth of the tests for graduate selection, ie sample sizes have been over 100 and reliability and validity estimates have been satisfactory (see Chapter 10).

- The tests you want to use are similar to those used by other companies selecting graduates and to those used by your major competitors who do not seem to be facing the level of 'wastage' problems that your organisation is facing.

In most commercial and other organisations, the chances of gaining support for change will be enhanced by proposals which estimate the financial benefit to be obtained. Ways of estimating the financial benefits that may be obtained from testing (and other selection methods) are explained by Dr Jeannette James in Appendix 8. Other things being equal, the cost benefits from selection procedures are highest when one or more of the following apply:

(a) the validity of the selection procedure is high
(b) the selection ratio is low, ie there is a large number of applicants to choose from, relative to the number of vacancies
(c) enough applicants are of good/reasonable quality
(d) employees (in the relevant job) vary greatly in worth to the organisation, ie performance varies significantly.

There are some other issues that may also need to be addressed, particularly if a selection procedure already exists and possible improvements are being considered. Examples might be:

- the acceptability of the procedure both to the applicants and those who are using the tests and other selection methods

- the extent to which candidates are learning from the experience of being assessed; in part this will depend on the feedback that assessors give them about their performance (see Chapter 3)

- the extent to which line managers are satisfied with the standard of those recruited; this can be particularly important if the managers cannot be directly involved in the recruitment of staff who will work for them, as might be the case in a nationally-run graduate recruitment programme

- the extent to which business leaders are satisfied with the results; although their satisfaction may be based on opinions and impressions rather than scientific evidence about reliability and validity, perceptions are reality and need to be managed accordingly.

If all these issues are taken into account in proposals that are made, recommendations to introduce tests are likely to succeed. But even then it is possible that recommendations may not be supported or may even be resisted. For example:

- The number of applicants and the number of vacancies may not seem to others to justify the costs of staff being trained to use tests; under these circumstances the case for using tests should be carefully costed and alternative strategies should be considered, such as the retention of a consultant or sharing the cost of selection with other companies through a group scheme.

- Questions may be raised about the fairness of tests, *vis-à-vis* applicants from ethnic minorities, those who do not match the prevailing sexual stereotype for the vacancy, and the disabled; such questions may be anticipated if it is proposed to use tests for selection in organisations keen to advance opportunities for minority groups, and careful background research with the test developers and publishers may be required to establish the fairness of the proposed procedures.

- The judgement that the use of tests will be beneficial may be challenged; until the tests have actually been used in a particular organisation and results followed up, it is impossible to demonstrate the worth of tests with absolute certainty and some may exploit this weakness in the case being put forward; explanations involving probability and other statistics may impress some but infuriate others. For example, people who failed the 11 plus, whose sons and daughters failed the 11 plus or those who feel that they were inappropriately placed during wartime or national service may be strongly opposed to testing. In contrast, others may be supportive because of their past successes in selections involving tests, or because they have found career guidance involving tests useful for their children, etc.

- Some may fear the consequences of better selection; for example, trainers may be concerned that courses may not be filled if higher selection standards are applied, while supervisors may fear the appointment of bright subordinates whom they will find difficult to manage.

So even if a case is technically sound there is no guarantee of proposals being accepted. Therefore some time should be spent seeking the views of those who may influence the decision and making sure the proposals embrace the points to which they are likely to be sympathetic and deal effectively with any objections. If written proposals are also to be presented orally it may be worth holding back a little information about the potential worth of tests in order to strengthen the case being made on the day.

Sometimes it is impossible to make a strong case, as when no proven tests exist for the type of vacancy to be filled. Resistance can also be strong for this or other reasons. One way forward can then be to get agreement to a trial in which the tests are administered at the time of selection but the results are not used. Later the test scores can be compared with performance as in a predictive validation study (see Chapter 10) and a decision about whether or not to use the tests for selection can be based on the results.

Organising testing

Assume that proposals for testing graduate entrants have been approved. A training course in the use of tests has been successfully completed (or the services of an occupational psychologist retained) and it has been decided to use the tests as part of an initial sift – that is, only those short-listed applicants who reach a satisfactory standard on the test will be invited to the final interviews. What preparations are necessary?

First, thought needs to be given to the likely response, offer and appointment rates. Precise numbers and types of vacancy can be difficult to forecast and may change at short notice according to the latest business plans for expansion or contraction, changes in staff turnover rates etc. In addition, when recruiting graduate entrants there is the problem of estimating how many of those accepting offers will actually start work and not withdraw their acceptance if a better offer arises. Such problems are rarely appreciated by applicants, who are understandably annoyed if they reply promptly to advertisements only to find that all vacancies have been filled. They are particularly annoyed if they are successful during the initial part of a selection procedure and then find out that all the vacancies are filled before they have the opportunity to attend the final part.

Whatever the difficulties in making accurate forecasts, administrators must persevere with the best estimates available and try to avoid major errors. For example, there is little point in inviting all applicants for initial tests if it will be impossible to interview all who are successful. On the other hand, if the number of initial applicants is too low and the numbers are then reduced because of the use of tests, the numbers being passed on to final interview may be insufficient. Past records may help to judge the numbers that should ideally be attracted, as may advice on the current state of affairs from careers officers, business contracts, advertising agencies, etc. It may be necessary to use suitable application forms (or design a supplement to an existing form) in order to sift on other relevant grounds if need be.

Applicants should be told in advance what the selection procedure will involve – perhaps in the job advertisement, but certainly when sending out application forms and job descriptions in response to enquiries. Ideally applicants should be sent handouts ahead of the procedure, which outline the kinds of tests to be used and give one or two example items for practice; they will then have time to seek further information from public libraries, from relatives and friends etc. The handouts should also describe the selection procedure as a whole and answer any questions commonly raised by applicants. Applicants should be warned to bring spectacles and hearing aids if they need them. Major employers such as the Post Office have printed leaflets for use in major recruitment programmes.

Testing should be carried out in groups of appropriate size; a test administrator should not normally test more than 20 people without assistance from other staff, though the precise number would depend on (i) the level of appointment and type of test being used; (ii) environmental factors, such as room size, and (iii) the testing materials available.

(i) *Level of appointment and type of test:* a few applicants can feel threatened by some kinds of testing – an example might be an applicant for a top management post who has never seen a personality questionnaire but who has heard criticisms from others; if testing is being carried out in circumstances in which good applicants are scarce, testing candidates individually or in pairs so that they can be greeted personally and given some individual attention is preferable to testing in larger groups in which individuals may feel anonymous.

(ii) *Environmental factors:* among the factors to be considered are:
the size of the room
adequate lighting
acoustics
quiet and free from interruption
comfortable seating
suitable work surface on which to rest papers etc
appropriate heating and ventilation.

(iii) *The testing materials available:* some tests comprise question booklets and separate answer sheets which enables the relatively expensive question booklets to be reused; the cost and availability of the booklets may influence the numbers to be tested at any one time.

Times for testing should relate to public transport times; consider late afternoon or evening sessions for those still studying; avoid clashes with examination dates. Check that there will not be any disruptions during testing, such as fire drills or major repairs in or near the building.

Make sure that applicants will be properly received and that there are suitable refreshment and toilet facilities.

Ask applicants to confirm their attendance – allow time for this and specify a contact point within the organisation.

As an introduction to the testing session, briefing about the use of tests should be repeated and expanded as part of the essential process of settling the candidate down. People generally feel more at ease and in control of a situation when they know what is going to happen and when; this applies to testing as much as to anything else, and it is important to continue to work to overcome any anxiety that individuals may feel when faced with psychological tests. Indeed, the selection of those who are to be handling the test sessions should focus, among other things, on the ability of the people concerned to establish rapport with the candidates and to deal with them in a sensitive and socially skilled way (see Chapter 1).

Reputable tests have detailed instructions on administration and these must be followed exactly. If the test instructions have to be read out to the candidates, the test administrator chosen must have a suitably clear and loud voice. If the testing session is a long one, time should be allowed for natural breaks.

If tests are being used as a sift, allow a sufficient period between testing and the final stage of selection for the tests to be marked and for those who are successful to be called forward: prior warning of the dates for the final stage of selection can allow the candidates to pencil the dates in their diaries.

Records should be kept of all test scores (preferably the answer sheets as well) to facilitate follow-up studies to check the worth of the tests and of the procedure as a whole.

Maintaining a large-scale testing programme

Some organisations use tests on a large scale. For example, Post Office Psychological Services supply up to 80,000 tests annually to over 200 locations throughout the UK.

When providing tests for use in decentralised organisations, instructions have to be issued on all the above points, and staff trained. The following points also have to be considered:

- the supply of tests from a central point; if this is done, stock control and distribution systems have to be implemented

- facilities for handling enquiries have to be established; for example, there may be enquiries from staff who need to administer tests and who have yet to attend formal training programmes

- there need to be systems for monitoring and inspecting the operation to ensure that good testing practices are being followed; steps will need to be taken to ensure that test materials are kept secure, samples of used test materials will need to be checked to make sure that they have been correctly scored, etc.

The following are illustrative of the kinds of problems that can arise in any large-scale testing operations:

- recommended tests may not be given (eg shortage of time, not considered suitable by local staff, fear that applicants may be put off by testing)

- other tests may be added or substituted (again both suitability and/or time required may be questioned by local staff)

- inappropriate norms may be used for grading

- confusion may have arisen over pass marks (eg when instructions stating that 'grade 4 is a pass' are interpreted by some to imply that all those obtaining any other grade should be rejected)

- local standards have been varied (lowered to fill vacancies or increased to keep numbers of applicants down) without regard to the requirements of the job and the future prospects for staff who are selected (see Chapters 5 and 8)

- senior managers without training in the use of the tests may demand unsupervised access to test materials and to test scores; some may even wish to keep records of the scores for further reference, with plans to look at the test scores when reviewing the performance of subordinates or even plans to evaluate the worth of the tests

- staff whose work involves the use of tests may fail to master their administration and interpretation, and may be unable to convince local managers of the need to follow recommended procedures

- test materials may not be returned when the testing staff move to other work; left unattended they may become compromised.

Testing individuals

There are a number of possible reasons for giving tests to an individual; for example, the individuals may be applicants for top management posts, or even people from widely differing levels and backgrounds whose placement in the organisation may not be working out.

To promote as positive an attitude as possible on the part of those tested, it helps to foster a co-operative or collaborative perspective on the exercise; and it assists greatly if a confidential feedback session on the results can be offered, so that there is something in it for the individual (see Chapter 10). If appropriate, it can be worth pointing out that selecting people who are wrong for a job or who are not going to perform satisfactorily is probably not going to do them any favours in the long run.

Evaluation

It is possible to evaluate selection methods after they have been introduced (see Chapter 10). Comparisons can then be made with:

- results that might have been expected by 'chance'
- results obtained by 'leading edge' organisations, by consultants etc.

However, there are some aspects of evaluation for which 'before' and 'after' comparisons can be useful – for example, there may be a wish to make a selection procedure more attractive to candidates as well as to improve it from a purely technical point of view.

Accordingly, the issue of evaluation should be addressed at this stage. All the objectives of the new (or revised) selection procedure should be noted and, if appropriate, current arrangements should be assessed or measured prior to changes being made.

Summary

Even if the case for introducing testing is technically sound, proposals to do so may be resisted. Accordingly, the case for testing must be prepared carefully and 'sold' to others who may also influence the decision.

Other factors affecting the success of testing range from winning the co-operation and interest of individual applicants to making sound administrative arrangements for larger groups. The choice of a suitable person to do the testing is particularly important (see Chapter 4).

8
Introducing tests for selection (III) Making and communicating decisions

Because of the vast number of tests available it is impossible to give detailed advice on the interpretation of scores on particular tests. What is possible is to give some basic principles that guide the use of test information in decision-making. They are:

- using aptitude tests
- using personality questionnaires
- combining results to increase predictive power
- the integration of results with other parts of the selection
- access to results
- giving feedback on results.

Using aptitude tests

Pencil and paper aptitude tests can be administered to groups of applicants. For this reason they are often given at an early stage in the selection process as an aid to 'sifting' the applicants and deciding which should be called to interviews or other stages of the procedure that are more time-consuming (see Chapter 5).

Used wisely, the strategy can have considerable commercial significance. For example, the use of tests as part of an initial sifting sometimes enables the Post Office to appoint one in every four applicants that it assesses in depth for executive posts; however, when sifting has not been possible, the proportion appointed can fall dramatically and occasionally senior staff have spent days interviewing unsuitable candidates and not making any appointments.

In order to sift, 'cut-off' points need to be established on the test or tests that are being used. This section describes how 'cut-offs' can be set and discusses some possible disadvantages of this strategy.

To illustrate the point, imagine that an employer is faced with a large number of applicants for a two-year youth training scheme in engineering. In order to sift fairly and minimise the chances of failure during training, the work is studied and a decision made to use a test of mechanical aptitude. It is agreed that a personnel manager should attend a training course in the use of such a test.

While attending the training course, the personnel manager is given the information in Table 2. Possible scores on the test range from 0 to 30, and based on a total sample (n) of 200 YTS applicants to four other employers the percentile ranks have been drawn up. (An individual's percentile score shows the percentage of applicants whose scores that individual has exceeded.)

Table 2

Mechanical aptitude test score	Percentile rank for applicant
30	95+
28–29	90
25–27	80
21–24	70
16–20	60
12–15	50
8–11	40
7	30
6	20
3–5	10
0–2	5

There are at least five ways in which the personnel manager may decide on a 'cut-off' for sifting in his or her own organisation:

- The first option is to press the test publishers for additional information about the use of the test elsewhere; this may yield recent information about the worth of the test being established for similar purposes.

- Second, it may be possible to get relevant information from local business contacts through Institute of Personnel and Development meetings etc; staff of local colleges involved in training may know of other companies using the same test; of course, if the test is used widely among local employers, its effectiveness could be reduced through applicants taking it several times and becoming practised (see Chapter 6).

- Third, it may be possible to test existing trainees whose performance is known; it is of course necessary to reassure those trainees that the test results would be used only as an aid to designing future selection procedures and will not affect their prospects; a potential problem here is that the existing trainees will not be as strongly motivated as they were at the time of selection and this may affect their test scores; further, the exercise will at best be a measure of concurrent rather than predictive validity (see Chapter 1).

- Fourth, a pragmatic decision could be made based on the numbers that can be accommodated in the final stages of selection and the likely final selection ratio; for example, it may be anticipated that one in six of those interviewed will be given job offers and that three of every five offered jobs will accept; the numbers to be 'passed' can then be calculated once all the applicants have been tested.

- Fifth, the test could be given to applicants without the results being taken into account initially; selection could take place on other grounds and then the progress of applicants followed up to see whether there is a relationship between test scores and performance and whether a 'cut-off' can be established; while this approach has the advantage of providing information about what happens to applicants with low test scores, attitudes to this strategy will vary; some may welcome an objective trial but others may not be happy with the idea of taking on low scorers and waiting to see if they fail!

The actual method chosen will depend on circumstances. Factors to be taken into account include the following:

- What numbers of applicants and vacancies exist? With 1,000 applicants and 100 vacancies the worth of the test can be checked on the intake for a single year; with 10 applicants and one vacancy decisions will have to be based on the experience of test designers and others.

- How effective are present selection methods? If they are good it may be possible to let things run while the worth of the test is established;

however, if urgent action is required arbitrary decisions may be necessary in the hope of improving the situation quickly.

- How many applicants are coming forward? Can the numbers be increased? If there are many vacancies and few applicants, the use of tests as a sift may make recruitment even more difficult.

- Can a minimum standard be established below which applicants are unlikely to succeed?

- Can a maximum score be established above which applicants may be too able and present problems because they are bored?

Mention has been made of the possibility of following up the performance of those already recruited; in order to build up numbers this might involve data about the recruitment of employees over several years, but care must be taken in doing this – for example, if the standards of performance expected of employees has changed radically over recent years, it would not be appropriate to include all performance ratings. Returning to the earlier example about youth trainees, imagine that the data in Table 3 were collected about the trainees who had taken the mechanical aptitude test, at the end of the two-year training. Given the data below, the cut-off might ideally be set at the score of 25, so that the chance of those selected finishing their training would be 95 per cent. However, this strategy would mean creaming off the very best of the applicants in terms of test scores, and it is important to check whether there are sufficient applicants to make this a practical proposition.

Table 3

Mechanical aptitude test score	Percentage of entrants completing training
25 and over	95
21–24	93
16–20	86
12–15	82
8–11	75
6–7	68
5 and below	45

In this example, the need to check is confirmed by looking back to Table 2. Taking only those who scored 25 and above would mean selecting the top 20 per cent of applicants, so to find 20 people who attained this level of performance on the test a pool of 100 candidates would be needed. Sometimes the term 'selection ratio' is used to summarise the situation. If only those scoring above 25 were taken on there would be a selection ratio of 0.20 (the ratio of the number to be taken on, 20, to the number of applicants, 100).

But what if there are fewer than 100 applicants? One possible way to fill the vacancies will be to reduce the cut-off score. Thus, if there are only 50 applicants and 20 trainees are again required, the selection ratio would be 20:50 or 0.40 as it would normally be expressed. To recruit 20 trainees from 50 applicants would mean that the crucial test score would be lowered to 16, as it can be seen that 59 per cent of applicants get a score of 15 or below, and 40 per cent get 16 or above. Going back to the data on the relationship between test scores and completion of training, the proportion of applicants getting a score of 16 or more that would be expected to finish the training would be 86 per cent.

In practice the cut-off score would have to be lowered still further to allow for the rejection of candidates who are unsuitable in other parts of the selection procedure. Although tests can be the most useful part of a selection procedure they should never be used alone.

Sometimes the need to fill vacancies may lower the pass mark to a level where the likely percentage of failures will be unacceptable. One way of dealing with such circumstances is to put additional effort into raising the numbers of applicants by, for example, more advertising; other alternatives might be to improve induction and other training, to redesign the work to make it less demanding, etc.

By contrast, some employers are currently faced with the problem of having large numbers of well-qualified people applying for relatively undemanding jobs. In the absence of data showing a clear statistical relationship between scores and the criterion, such employers sometimes assume that 'you can't have too much of a good thing' and cut-off points are raised higher and higher. However, the assumption does not always hold; for example, several studies have shown that managerial performance correlates with intellectual test scores only up to a point; beyond this point, very high test scores do not seem to be associated with superior managerial effectiveness.

Quite apart from this kind of finding, the blind pursuit of high test scores may simply result in the selection of a group of people who are over-qualified for the job in question, and who will quickly become frustrated, bored or dissatisfied and are then likely to leave.

Using personality questionnaires

Although the examples given so far have been based on aptitude tests, the same issues apply when considering the results of personality questionnaires. Indeed, the picture here is even more complex. There are two broad ways in which such measures can be used. The first is in a holistic fashion, trying to get an overall picture of the individual by looking at the pattern of scores and examining the interrelationships between the different traits. So, for example, a manager given a personality questionnaire may have produced a profile that indicates high levels of emotionality and aggression. This does not necessarily mean, however, that the individual concerned will frequently display these dispositions in an overt way. We might find that other scores suggest that he is actually a very restrained person who exercises firm self-control, and that he has a high level of objectivity and insight, indicating that he is unlikely to be all that easily offended. Thus, only by taking account of the wider pattern of personality scores can the implications be seen for how the person will behave.

This approach to interpreting personality data is sometimes called the clinical method, as it reflects the way a psychologist might use the information in trying to gain a deeper understanding of the personality of one particular individual. To be effective, it calls for considerable skill and experience, along with an underlying knowledge of the psychology of personality. The alternative to this, which is generally used in organisations, is to take a more statistical, even mechanistic approach. Here, the objective is to avoid having to do much actual interpretation of the personality scores, and instead to be guided by the empirical relationships already established between the scores and various criteria of job success. The aim is to select people who have the kind of personality questionnaire scores that are associated with effective performance – irrespective of any possible interrelationships there might be between individual dimension scores. There are several versions of this way of using personality data, involving cut-off scores, 'danger zones', and profile matching.

Taking the first of these, *cut-offs*, similar dangers exist as were mentioned in relation to ability scores. Suppose, for instance, that a personality questionnaire has an emotionality scale, and that an organisation has found (or believes) that high scores on the scale – indicative of high anxiety levels – are associated with poor performance. It might be tempted to introduce a cut-off score, to screen out applicants who are anxiety-prone or unstable. But what about people who score at the other extreme on this dimension, very low scorers who seem to lack emotions and feelings? They may be highly insensitive and tactless, unable to empathise with those around them; presumably the organisation would not want to recruit many of them (particularly in some jobs), yet by using a simple cut-off it would fail to select them out.

An increasingly common way of dealing with this problem is to establish so-called *danger zones*, which in effect are upper and lower cut-offs. A company might, on the basis of the correlations it has found between some personality measure scores and job performance, identify that people falling below a specific level on any one dimension are unlikely to be successful. Yet it also recognises – perhaps on a common sense basis as much as anything – that extreme scores in either direction are probably contra-indicative of success. So it establishes a range of scores within which candidates are acceptable, but above or below which they are rejected. This is an increasingly common method, and one that is both flexible and relatively easy to use. It is not without its problems and dilemmas, however. For example, how does one compare a candidate who has fallen inside a danger zone on, say, two of the eight scores and who looks very good on the other six, with a candidate whose scores are only just within the acceptable range on all eight dimensions? There is no easy answer to this – it is a judgement call.

The third type of statistically based approach to using personality questionnaires involves the development of *profiles* for specific jobs or occupational groups. Scores on personality inventories are often put together to produce a profile chart which shows the individual's position on each dimension in relation to the average score and in terms of the distribution of scores as a whole. This is a very popular way of summarising the basic facts. The background against which the person's score is portrayed may be the norms built up for that organisation or they may be the norms as supplied by the test producer in the test manual. Sometimes, as in Cattell's 16PF, the well-known personality questionnaire, there is quite a range of profiles available showing the score patterns for different occupational groups.

The profiles appear so convenient and helpful that it is easy to overlook some important considerations in using them. The first is that to be of any real worth, the norms presented in the profile must be based on adequate sample sizes; groups of 40 or so are just not large enough to be confident in the stability of the data; groups of at least 100 are essential and groups of 200 or more are to be preferred.

The second danger is that the norms used may not be appropriate. For example, it might be most appropriate to compare graduate applicants for general management with each other and/or applicants 12 months earlier; to compare them either with those actually taken on 12 months earlier or with graduates applying for sales posts could severely mislead.

The third danger is of thinking that the profile represents a picture of what is desirable and effective in terms of personal qualities for that group rather than simply what is typical. Profiles from groups of scientific researchers can illustrate that this is unwise. On the 16PF, these groups can be characterised by, amongst other things, tender-mindedness (or emotional sensitivity). But in studies that have focused on an index of effectiveness, in this instance the number of publications the scientist produces, it has been found that the more effective members of this group are actually characterised by tough-mindedness.

What occupational group profiles present is a picture of what is typical of people who have stayed in a particular job and perhaps adjusted to it. However, their experiences of the job might well have affected their replies and hence their profiles. So one problem is that group profiles reflect concurrent validity rather than the preferable predictive validity (see Chapter 1). Further, group profiles often do not differentiate between those in the group who are performing well and those who are not. It is of course possible to develop separate profiles for the successful and unsuccessful sub-groups and this more detailed information is required for effective selection decisions.

In this section, the main approaches to using personality questionnaire results have been outlined (a refinement of the statistical approach, using regression analysis, will be mentioned in the next section). What was described as the clinical approach relies heavily on the expertise of the person doing the interpretation. Its advantages are that it uses all the information yielded by the questionnaire, and that it can provide a richer and deeper understanding of personality than can the more mechanistic techniques described above. However, because it relies on interpretation, this approach is also inevitably more subjective in nature, and where there is more subjectivity, there is greater scope for error. This is the main advantage of the statistically based use of personality questionnaires – it minimises subjectivity and reduces the need for skilled interpretation, thus rendering it more widely usable.

Given that there is no one 'right' way of using personality inventory information, and all the alternatives have their strengths and weaknesses, what is the personnel practitioner to do? Much will depend on the purpose the questionnaire is being put to, and on the available level of training and expertise in the use of the instrument concerned. In general, the 'danger zones' approach will probably be more appropriate in large-scale selection exercises, and the clinical, interpretative approach will be needed when dealing with individual cases. An extremely valuable compromise between the two is where personality scores are used to highlight areas of doubt about candidates (perhaps because of some scores falling outside the acceptable range) and to raise other questions or hypotheses concerning their personality make-up which can then be followed up by, and probed in, an interview. We will return to this matter shortly when discussing the integration of test results with other parts of the selection procedure.

Finally, while discussing the use of personality questionnaires, it is worth raising some of the more general issues about them that have been debated rather publicly in the last few years. Probably the widest currency (in the media, at least) has been given to the allegations made by the staff of one commercial consultancy company that personality measures of this kind were of little real use in assessing people for jobs. The basis for this claim (in part statistical) was evaluated by a number of the leading academic and business experts in the field – none of whom had a vested interest in the sense of being involved in the production of personality questionnaires – and the results were published in *Personnel Management* (September 1991). Their collective view was that these claims lacked any substance, and that they should be dismissed.

More constructive, however, has been the discussion of the use of ipsative versus normative personality measures. This is a somewhat technical issue, but briefly it revolves around two different approaches to personality measurement. Whereas normative test scales are independent (thus, for example, your score on the anxiety scale is not affected in any way by how you answered questions on the sociability scale), ipsative test scales are not. The latter, in effect, invite the respondent to make choices between the relative strengths of different personality qualities in their make-up. In other words, they do not compare the individual with other people, they produce a picture of how dominant different tendencies are within a single person. The 16PF is an example of a normative test, while the Concept Four version of the OPQ® is an ipsative one. Both approaches have their merits, but the problem comes when they are used interchangeably, particularly where an ipsative test score is used to compare people as if it were a normative one. A full description of the two approaches is beyond the scope of this book, and the reader is referred to Johnson, Saville and Fletcher (1989) for a succinct look at the question. However, it is certainly important to find out which type a personality questionnaire is, in deciding whether it is appropriate to your needs.

Combining results to increase predictive power

The complexity of most jobs makes it unlikely that a single quality will determine success and therefore that a single test will be adequate to assess applicants' suitability. The question then arises of how to combine tests together into a battery. One way is to use multiple cut-offs, so that the tests are taken in a series, with only those individuals who have exceeded the critical score on the first test going on to take the second, and so on. In practice this is a rather cumbersome process and likely to be used only in a limited range of circumstances (generally where there is a multiple-stage screening procedure).

The other way of using tests together is sometimes called the composite score method. This involves the use of complex statistical techniques – multiple correlation and regression analysis – that are beyond the scope of the present discussion; see Lewis (1985) for a fuller description. In effect, this method takes the individual correlations established between each test and the criterion, and between the tests themselves. It finds what is the best combination of test information for predicting performance and other criteria and yields a set of weights that can be used in future, which gives the correct emphasis to each piece of test data to maximise the accuracy of the prediction. The composite score approach to combining tests often shows that the power of a battery of tests is much greater than the individual test validities might indicate. Several separate tests may have correlations with the criterion in the 0.1–0.2 range, but a composite score may produce a correlation of 0.4 or more.

This approach can also be used to identify which particular traits within a personality questionnaire are the most important in terms of prediction. For example, it may be found that administrative ability, drive, work commitment, emotional stability and sociability, as measured by a personality inventory, all correlate more or less equally with some indices of sales success. However, it may well be that there is some degree of intercorrelation between these scales. The use of regression analysis can identify which of them is most important in predicting success, and how they should be individually weighted and combined to yield the best prediction. It could quite easily be that work commitment and sociability are the main predictors, with emotional stability adding a lesser (but still useful) amount of predictive power and the other two trait scores being redundant. How is it that these last two – administrative ability and drive – could be of no use when the original analysis showed that they seemed to correlate well enough with the criterion of sales success? Simply because they both correlated strongly with the work commitment scale scores, and their relationship with sales success was entirely due to this, rather than to anything extra they added for themselves.

The above discussion assumes that an organisation has some data on the relationship between test scores and whatever it is they are trying to predict. Often, that is not the case, so there is no opportunity to find out what the optimum weighting for each test should be. This should not deter them from using a battery of tests and combining their results together on a more intuitive basis to build up a picture of the candidate. Evidence shows that while this is not as effective a way of using the information to predict future performance as is statistical analysis, it can still produce impressive results (Bentz, 1985; Moses, 1985). The range of abilities and qualities that generally need to be considered is in itself a convincing reason for the use of a battery of tests, providing that the battery does not become so large that it is more a test of endurance than of anything else.

Integrating results with other parts of a selection procedure

When the main stage of the assessment is reached, a number of questions arise. First, if tests have yet to be given, should they be given before or after an interview? The answer is that they are best administered before any interview, so that the results can act as a source of hypotheses that interviewers can probe and test in the interview. Any marked traits or deficiencies might be singled out in this way, especially in relation to personality characteristics. Also, any discrepancy between the level of intellectual potential (as shown by the tests) and the individual's level of achievement should be the source of close scrutiny. There is a counter argument that maintains the test results should not be available before the interview so that the interviewers are not biased in their judgements by the information. There is some force in this but overall the balance is definitely in favour of using the results to guide the interview – there are apt to be a lot of queries hanging in the air afterwards if they are not.

Another issue is how much weight to give to the test scores compared to other sources of assessment data, such as academic record, references, interviewers' ratings and so on, and in practice some users place too much weight on test scores and others too little. The evidence on the validity of tests compared with the validity of interview and other information is such as to make a strong case for putting the greatest weight on the psychometric test results (McCormick and Ilgen, 1985). The interview, as it is normally carried out and on its own, has repeatedly been shown to lack both reliability and validity. Much the same can be said of the value of references. Although some studies of references have shown good validity (eg university references about graduates sent to the Civil Service Commission) this cannot be assumed. Academic record and other background facts about the person can contribute significantly to accurate prediction when treated statistically and put together in the form of a 'biodata' questionnaire – though this is just mechanistic prediction and does not say anything about the individual as such. By themselves, facts about academic achievements have proved very variable predictors and generalisations are particularly difficult to make. In part this is due to the fact that differences in grades can reflect small differences in marks, that there are different pass rates in different subjects, that there are different Examination Boards and syllabuses, and so on. Psychometric tests commonly predict future performance better than do academic results.

The wisest strategy is to gather assessment information from a number of sources rather than to rely completely on any one. None, including psychological tests, is perfect or anywhere near it. Where discrepancies in the findings from these sources arise, they need to be investigated thoroughly. In general, though, the test data are likely to prove the more objective and predictive.

From all that has been said so far on the subject of using tests in decision-making, it should be apparent that there are considerable dangers in trying to interpret results in an entirely mechanistic fashion. But this is precisely what some assessment reports generated on microcomputers do; the test or questionnaire data are fed in and the machine produces a series of statements that appear to be justified by the individual scores rather than groups of factors or the total profile. This is discussed in more detail in Chapter 12.

Access to results

The increasing use of psychological tests brings with it the danger of the abuse of the information they provide.

Controlling the access to that information is one way of reducing the danger. Ideally, test results should be available only to the individual assessed (in the course of a properly conducted feedback session, of which more anon), to a personnel manager trained in their use, and beyond that on a limited 'need to know' basis. Assuming that the personnel department is arranging the assessment, any access to the results given to line managers – who are likely to be untrained in testing – should be carefully monitored and guided by the personnel manager concerned. Failure to do this is likely to lead to a fair range of horrors, from excessive reliance on the findings (and probably wrongly interpreted for good measure) to complete disregard of them. There should certainly be no question of copies of test results or the reports written on the basis of them being held anywhere other than in the personnel department and access should be restricted to accredited users. Completed answer sheets and profiles are confidential documents and must be treated as such.

How long should the results of tests be kept and referred to? A rule of thumb on this would be to say the test data have a 'shelf life' of five years and no more than that. People and circumstances change, and to dig out test results from 15 years ago when making a decision about an individual – which has been known to happen – is neither fair nor sensible. Personality data will be more prone to variation over time than will ability scores, although over a very long period there may well be a tendency for verbal ability to improve while other ability scores decrease somewhat. There will be big individual differences in the extent of change over time, some people showing marked changes and some virtually none. The only safe option is to stop using the data after five years and, if the need arises, administer a fresh set of tests. However, data more than five years old should be kept as a source of information about the worth of long-term procedures, such as identification of potential top managers among graduate entrants.

If tests are being used as the sole basis of sifting, a five-year gap would seem to be far too long and a much shorter interval would seem appropriate. For example, the Post Office allows existing employees seeking promotion to attempt tests twice within a two-year period so that applicants do not feel that too much depends on their performance on a single occasion.

Giving feedback on results

Throughout this book there has been a great deal of emphasis on the reactions of the person taking the test and on the need to make the experience as acceptable and as stress-free as possible. This is particularly important when internal applicants are being assessed, since good feedback can help to sustain the motivation of those who have been unsuccessful. However, there is growing recognition that feedback to external candidates should help to make the procedure more attractive to them. Further, one of the surest ways of gaining honesty in answering questionnaires is for the candidate to know that there will be some feedback.

Ideally, feedback should be given by someone trained both in testing and counselling – it requires counselling skill to present results that are not always very positive in such a manner that the individual concerned is both accurately informed of them and still able to maintain motivation and self-esteem; see Fletcher (1985, 1986) for further discussion of this.

If at all possible, the feedback should be treated as a confidential discussion so that it does not become an extension of the assessment process in the eyes of the candidate. A fairly common approach to sessions of this kind is to start by seeking the candidate's views and feelings about the tests, then to go through them one by one – always checking that the tests being talked about at each stage are recalled by the individual and that he or she is given the opportunity to comment on the results.

When the basic test data have been conveyed, the discussion moves on to interpreting them in terms of their implications for the individual's behaviour and relationships at work, development needs, career progression and aspirations, and so on. The more the candidate can be encouraged to participate in this interpretation and discussion, the better it is likely to be. It will be in the organisation's interests as well that employees or potential employees who have undergone psychometric assessment should be able to use the information obtained in seeking to improve future performance.

It is sometimes possible to give feedback on some aspects of performance (eg test and questionnaire results) during an assessment or immediately afterwards, and this can increase motivation to attend. But there is a strong case for delaying most of the feedback until the outcome of the assessment is known, particularly for internal applicants. The feedback will be much more meaningful if related to the new job or to the prospects for those who have not been successful.

Other options

In Chapter 5 there was information about the large-scale testing programmes carried out by major employers such as the Post Office and

Civil Service. The question arises as to whether, and in what ways, feedback can be given to external candidates, particularly when very large numbers of applicants are involved and a very large amount of time might be required.

In part the strategy of the testing organisation regarding feedback will depend on the type of test used. If, for example, applicants have attempted a test designed to measure computer programming aptitude which has been used as a first sift, a letter telling applicants that they had not reached a sufficiently high standard to move on to the next stage of the procedure might at first seem adequate. However, it would be helpful to candidates to know whether their rejection was because there were too many candidates with higher scores or whether they simply did not meet the minimum standards; from the point of view of the candidate this could make the difference between trying for programming work elsewhere and making applications for a different kind of work.

Some candidates like to ask questions of someone trained in testing and counselling skills in order to obtain any additional information (eg was the failure 'borderline'? Is the aptitude test widely used?).

While contact by letter or telephone might suffice if a particular skill is being tested, complications may arise if either a range of qualities are being tested or if the candidate has taken part in a more complex procedure such as an assessment centre.

If a range of qualities has been tested, there is more likelihood of the applicant being 'hurt' by the knowledge that he or she has failed to reach the required standard. It is one thing for a person to learn that he or she has not got the aptitude for a particular job, quite another for the person to receive information which suggests that he or she has little potential for any job! However, simply to avoid giving feedback does not help the candidate who could benefit by learning about areas of relative strength and being reminded that there are many jobs for which the particular tests used would not be relevant. Again, the telephone number of a good trained contact person might be given; an alternative would be for some insight into the results to be passed indirectly to the candidates via trained counsellors and careers advisers with a background in testing. A third possibility is to prepare an appropriate report for the individual using a computer-based 'expert system' (see Chapter 12).

If the candidate has attended an assessment centre, the potential problems in giving feedback would seem to be even greater because of the very detailed information that has been collected. However, the demand for feedback from the candidates is also likely to be high because of the time and, in some cases, personal information they have given. Feedback using the kinds of strategies described above might again be helpful.

A form of feedback that can do more harm than good is simply to send a written copy of the test results or of a report on them to the individual without any amplification. Apart from the fact that things can look a little stark in print, the person concerned is almost certainly untrained in testing and knows next to nothing about what the scores really mean or how the interpretations are arrived at. The scope for misunderstanding is formidable, and there is a good chance that the recipient will be upset by some of what is said. With no opportunity to seek elucidation or to explore the implications of the results with someone who is properly trained, the individual may be worse off than if no feedback had been given at all.

A totally different argument against giving feedback is that it might give candidates more opportunity to question the decisions that have been made. However, if the procedures have been professionally designed and run by trained staff they should have no difficulty in justifying their point of view.

Summary

Although tests are often used as a means of sifting applicants to decide who will attend the final and more time-consuming parts of the selection procedure, considerable attention may need to be paid to establishing the cut-offs and there is no single best way of doing this; indeed there are a number of pitfalls to be avoided and the actual method chosen will depend on very particular circumstances.

There are also potential pitfalls when using profiles from personality questionnaires; in particular, profiles from occupational groups are often based on all those doing a particular job, and not just those who are successful at it. The pros and cons of the statistical and holistic approaches to using personalilty questionnaire results are discussed.

Ways of combining test results to increase their predictive power have been outlined, and ways of integrating test results with other parts of the selection procedure have been suggested. On the balance of things, it is recommended that interviewers should know the test scores of applicants before they interview so that the reasons for any apparent discrepancies can be probed.

Finally, the control of access to test scores is strongly recommended.

It is also recommended that scores should not be stored for longer than five years unless follow-up studies are planned. The importance of giving the principle of feedback to applicants, particularly those already working within the organisation, is discussed and ways of doing this are described.

9
Testing top managers

Much of the early work with tests involved their use on a large scale, either to select staff for government, the military or for groups of vacancies such as apprentices or clerical workers. However, in more recent times, there has been increasing use of testing in connection with (a) the selection of top managers and (b) their development. For example, the multinational company ITT put in place an executive assessment programme for its most senior people way back in 1959, and this acted as a model for many other applications of psychometric testing at this level for some while after.

The selection of top managers

In our view, work on the selection of top managers should be approached in the same way as any other kind of selection assignment; that is, it is essential to obtain a clear understanding of the work to be done and the issues to be faced; it is also important to learn about the history of the post (have others tried and failed and, if so, why?) and about the skills and development needs of those who will report to the post-holder; appreciation of the culture of the organisation and whether and how it needs to be developed or changed is another key issue if a successful appointment is to be made.

Given a good understanding of the vacancy and of the qualities required in a successful candidate, appropriate selection procedures need to be identified. At this level we think it important to assess whether applicants can demonstrate their ability to do the job as a whole, since top management is about using combinations of knowledge and skill rather than using individual skills on their own. (If you are in any doubt about this assertion, consider whether you would fly with a 'pilot' who knew about aircraft and airports, about engines and fuel, about navigation and communication, and about instruments and controls, but who had never actually flown before.)

Tests of the kind described elsewhere in this book can be used in a number of ways including:

- to help identify the kind of manager required
- to help shortlist the applicants
- as part of the main selection proccdure
- to review the most promising candidates.

Testing to help identify the kind of manager required

In theory, tests could be used to help identify the kind of manager required. This could be of value if, for example, a management team is not pulling together. Asking the management team to complete tests and questionnaires may shed some light on team dynamics (or lack of them) and the management qualities required to move the team forward. (The information could also be used as part of a team-building event once the new manager has been appointed – see below.)

In practice, it is our experience that tests are seldom used in this way. One reason is that there is often pressure to fill the vacancy without too much delay. Another is that at least some members of the team may be applying for the vacant top job and, in situations where access to a range of tests is limited, there may be reluctance to use the same tests for both 'diagnostic' purposes and for the subsequent selection procedure. Whatever the reason, we believe that that more use could be made of tests for 'diagnostic' purposes, and we believe that time spent in this way may increase the accuracy of subsequent selection.

Testing to help shortlist the applicants

Some top management posts attract hundreds of applicants. However, careful preliminary work on the nature of the vacancy and the sort of person required to fill it may mean that shortlisting is relatively easy – for example, it may be decided that certain kinds of experiences and achievements are essential and only candidates with these experiences need be shortlisted.

At other times the vacancy may be one which could be filled by people from a wide variety of backgrounds – an example might be the post of chief executive of a small business or charity. A systematic approach to shortlisting could involve testing, but if the some of the candidates are to be met individually we would suggest that a variety of techniques should be used reflecting the key requirements of the vacant post; in the case of the chief executive of the small business or charity these might include:

- making a presentation about how to take the business or charity forward, and answering questions

- completing relevant tests or questionnaires

- an interview to discuss career history, aims and ambitions etc.

There are other possibilities, eg asking applicants to complete a business case study, but a compromise needs to be struck between the information ideally required and the length of meeting appropriate at this preliminary stage. Often it is felt that two hours of the applicant's time is the practical limit.

Testing as part of the main selection procedure

There are wide differences in the selection procedures for top managers. In some organisations, appointments are made by the chairman or chief executive and only the closest advisers even know of the vacancy. Possible applicants are discreetly 'tapped on the shoulder'.

In these circumstances it may well be possible to incorporate testing into the assessment procedure which might be along the following lines:

- a business case-study requiring a written report; questions to be asked about the report

- a presentation about how to take the business or charity forward, again answering questions

- completing relevant tests and questionnaires

- one or more interviews to discuss career history, professional or technical skills, managerial skills etc.

In contrast, a few organisations are completely 'open' about all their top appointments. This gives them the opportunity to bring candidates together as a group to compare their performance directly. Possible advantages of doing so are:

- to see whether candidates can display interpersonal and other skills in practice

- to be able to relate behaviour and performance with other aspects of the selection procedure such as test results; this can indicate whether applicants have a good understanding of their abilities and development needs, the way that they come across to others, etc.

In practice, group activities of this kind may yield relatively little information because the participants are so 'polished' in their interpersonal skills as to give little away. There is the further complication that it is normal to treat applications in the strictest confidence and this cannot be guaranteed if the candidates are to meet each other. Accordingly, if it is wished that the candidates should meet, we believe that they should be told of the proposed arrangements in advance.

Testing to assess the most promising candidates

Many organisations believe that they have the resources and expertise to identify the strongest applicants, particularly among their existing staff. This may be on the basis of track record in the organisation, or even on the basis of performance on the kinds of procedures outlined above, etc. However, some residual doubts may remain, of which examples may be the following questions:

- Can the individual cope with further promotion, or might this be one step too far?

- How does this person compare with other staff at the same level?

For these reasons, independent assessments by occupational psychologists or other consultants are sometimes sought as a final check before a key appointment is made. Typically, assessment processes at this level involve a battery of tests covering cognitive abilities and personality, as well as an in-depth interview. It would normally be carried out be a very experienced assessor, and last four to six hours (often this is the maximum amount of time available, and even that may be hard to arrange for people in demanding senior roles). Obviously, the level of difficulty of the cognitive tests used and the norm groups for the measures have to be chosen to be appropriate for top-level management. The resulting assessment report may be structured in terms of the specific competencies relevant to the job, or focus on particular queries raised about a candidate, or take a more general view of the individual. An example of such a senior level assessment report is given in Appendix 10.

One of the main reasons for having this assessment done by consultants external to the organisation, apart from any possible lack of such expertise internally, is political. It is not usually considered acceptable for a potential member of top management to go through such a sensitive and probing procedure conducted by someone who may soon be one of their subordinates. Also, experienced external consultants will be able to benchmark the assessment against industry standards at this level of seniority, and they should also have the credibility to handle the feedback to the candidate in a manner that is acceptable to him or her.

Case-studies

Six short case-studies follow to illustrate some of the issues that can arise in the selection of top managers.

Case-study 1

Around the time that the first edition of this book was published, a consultancy organisation approached a major employer claiming that they had a new method of selecting top managers. Each candidate was asked to look at drawings through a tachistoscope (apparatus resembling a camera shutter) and to describe what was seen. It was argued that 'good' managers would describe all the features of the drawing, whereas 'poor' managers would ignore aspects of the drawing that they did not expect to be there. The test had been based on the principle of perceptual defence – that because of the mass of information that we receive, our attention has to be selective, and this selectivity can mislead or distort. In addition to this method, candidates were also interviewed at length.

A psychologist who had expert knowledge of perceptual defence was asked to comment on the technique. She expressed surprise that the tachistoscope was always working at the same speed and that no attempt was made to calibrate each individual's speed of vision before starting the test. She could find no evidence of insight arising from the technique in the sample assessment reports that she was given, nor was she given any independent evidence of the worth of the technique in the selection of managers.

While this cannot be regarded as a comprehensive review of the technique, it raises the question as to whether all methods used to select top managers are valid. The same sorts of question can be raised about the use of graphology in management assessment, the evaluation of graphology being further complicated by the fact that most practitioners in the UK belong to one of three different schools of graphology with contrasting approaches and interpretations.

Case-study 2

A major commercial organisation planned to reorganise. It invited leading consultants to say how they would help to assess existing managers to decide which managers should be appointed to the top jobs in the new organisation.

One consultancy organisation proposed to make the assessments on the basis of reasoning tests and personality questionnaires alone; they did not see any reason to take the experience and business competence of the managers into account.

They were not successful in their tender for the work. The tender went to a rival consultancy organisation which used a variety of assessment techniques, including a business case-study, group discussions, a mock press interview, individual interviews, and tests and questionnaires. The work was well received and repeated elsewhere in the group.

The original organisation subsequently changed its approach to that of its successful rival and has recently won work from a different part of the group.

Case-study 3

An applicant for a top post was asked to complete a well-known personality questionnaire as part of the selection procedure. The result was a profile which suggested that he was a well-balanced and rounded individual who would be well suited to the particular vacancy and to the organisation. He was offered, and accepted, the appointment.

The results have been somewhat 'mixed'. On the one hand the person concerned has achieved a great deal and has taken on further responsibility. On the other hand, aspects of his behaviour and style have been the subject of adverse comment. Those who know him well feel that he is unable to adhere consistently to the high standards that he seeks in others – in other words, the personality questionnaire results reflect how he believes he behaves, not how he actually behaves.

Personality questionnaires are now widely used, and some managers will have taken them (and received feedback) on many occasions. As a result they may be able to answer the questions in ways that produce profiles which are compatible with the job requirements. Indeed, in subsequent discussions about their profiles, they may be able to go on to describe behaviour which gives credence to their replies. However, there is evidence that some bright and articulate managers are learning how best to reply to the questionnaires and to the interview questions rather than addressing and changing their day-to-day behaviours.

Case-study 4

An applicant for a top marketing post in a successful consultancy organisation had an exceptional career history, having gained rapid promotion in a world-class business in the financial services sector.

Discussion of her replies to a well known personality questionnaire identified some key qualities – that she was impatient, that she could not suffer fools, that she preferred to invest in people who could learn rapidly.

The consultancy was run by two principals with complementary qualities; both were finding it difficult to change and develop their working habits and behaviours and, at times, each could be extremely critical of the other.

Although the candidate had much to offer, she was not offered an appointment by the consultancy. One principal seemed to see her as a potential threat; the other decided not to force the issue.

Case-study 5

Sometimes test results do not confirm existing impressions of a candidate. This may be a little unwelcome or hard to accept, but it does not automatically mean that the tests are wrong.

A telecommunications company asked an external consultant to assess an applicant for a director-level post. The test results were surprisingly negative, particularly on the ability tests. 'These results can't be right' was the company verdict – 'he's got a wonderful track record'. They asked that he be re-tested, which he was, but with the same poor performance. The company was perplexed, and was considering disregarding the test result, when it emerged that the individual concerned had a drink problem, and quite a long-lasting one. The first reference checks had not picked this up. It was beginning to affect his intellectual functioning, which was reflected in the test results.

Case-study 6

This is an example of how important it is to try to maintain appropriate levels of confidentiality in relation to top-level assessments, and also to make sure that those who do see them have the necessary guidance or experience to be able to understand them.

A financial services organisation commissioned an occupational psychologist to assess a candidate for the post of IT director. The assessment report was duly sent to the personnel director, as a confidential document. He then circulated the report around several other managers within the organisation, without further explanation. They had no experience of such assessment reports and no frame of reference to guide their interpretation of what they were reading. In these circumstances, considerable misunderstandings can arise, and a particularly unfortunate consequence of this was that one of the line managers read out the report over the phone to the head-hunter who had proposed the candidate. The result was that a very garbled and inaccurate account went back to the candidate before he had attended for his formal feedback session which, not surprisingly, left him feeling rather upset – partly because of the misinterpretation and partly because of the lack of control of access to this sensitive material about him.

The development of top managers

Tests can be used to help top managers to develop. This can be done on an individual basis or with a group of managers. Sometimes the group will be one that works together, while at other times the group may comprise relative or complete strangers.

Feedback is essential if managers are to develop in this way; whether successful or not, it gives them the opportunity to reflect on how they may be coming across to others, in terms of their test profiles, their actual behaviour, or both. Ideally, they should aim to improve their management and other behaviour, rather than use the feedback to improve the way that they come across in assessments.

Testing and individual development
There are many possible ways in which individual managers may require development. Some may need to develop particular technical skills (eg non-finance managers may need to develop an understanding of finance) while others may need to develop in the area of general management or of business strategy.

It is important that these needs are correctly identified and prioritised; at a minimum this should involve the individual and his or her line manager, but may also involve an experienced mentor from within or outside the organisation.

Testing and team development
Tests can provide insight into team behaviour and performance. For example, questionnaires which help to assess the likely style of individual team members can help to identify areas in which individuals might clash, areas in which the team as a whole may have little or no interest, and so on. However, it must be remembered that such questionnaires depend on the self-perceptions of the team members; if these are not accurate, there is the further question of how individuals can be helped to see themselves more accurately. Skilled facilitation may be required

if individual views are to change positively and the team is to move forward.

The role of testing in other approaches to development

Some approaches to development involve a combination of individual and group work. One such approach, called 'development workshops', has been developed by the British Post Office for its top managers. The workshops have seven features, the combination of which is believed to be unique.

The seven features are:

1 The development of an overall 'model' to help people to take stock of themselves and to produce an individual development plan for the future. All the elements of the workshop are clearly related to the 'model'.

2 There is work for the participants and their line managers to do before attending the first of two workshop sessions so that they can get the best out of the time that they spend at the first workshop. An example is the 'learning styles questionnaire' designed by Honey and Mumford – participants are offered a personal report from Alan Mumford on their learning styles.

3 Attendance of the participant's line manager on the first day of the first workshop. This gives the opportunity for the line manager and participant to compare views about (a) competencies required in the participant's current job (b) the participant's strongest and weakest competencies, and (c) competencies likely to be required in top Post Office managers in the future.

4 Use of 'career architect' materials. Based on US research into generic management competencies, the following materials are used: (a) 67 cards, each describing a management competency and giving indications of how the competency might be 'over-used'; (b) 19 cards describing 'career stoppers' and books linking each competency with development activities. 'Career stoppers' are behaviours which have been shown to hold people back if they are not addressed.

5 Use of action learning sets; participants work in action learning sets on at least three occasions, sharing plans and ideas and offering each other support and constructive criticism. The sets are facilitated by leading external consultants to give additional insight and experience and to ensure confidentiality.

6   There is an interval of some six weeks between the two parts of the development workshop; this is to allow time for the participants to clarify information about their competencies, their values, possible development opportunities etc. A panel of experts is available to offer help and support on an individual basis, if required. It is at this stage that tests may be used to help individual managers either to clarify their development needs, or to clarify possible plans for the future, or a combination of both.

7   Participants meet for a further 30 hours to share the work that they have done when 'taking stock' and to start to prepare their plans for the future. By the end of the workshop they are expected to have drafted an individual development plan. Following the workshop they are asked to finalise the plan with their line manager and to send it to the director of management development for the Post Office.

Summary

Tests can make a contribution to the selection and development of top managers, and in individual instances can be the source of considerable insight. However, in general the successful selection and development of top managers depends on a large number of issues and on their ability to display evidence of combinations of knowledge, skill and behaviour; accordingly the importance of individual test results should not be overstated. While, at their best such test results can help to identify issues and to crystallise issues and themes arising from other information, there is little to be said in favour of the common practice of using test results in isolation, and much to be said against it.

10
Evaluating a testing programme

This chapter draws together some of the issues raised elsewhere in the book and considers them in more detail:

- How can the worth of a test be assessed, ie is it valid?

- Does the test discriminate fairly?

- Has the testing been worthwhile financially? (Benefits, costs and potential problems).

Once again, the main focus of comments will be on the process of selection.

Checking the worth of a test

Validity is perhaps the most important factor to take into account when evaluating a test, for if the test does not measure what it claims to measure the procedure is pointless.

In an ideal world, the validity of the test or tests chosen would have been already established during a number of similar applications, and the potential confirmed by trials in which the tests were administered at the time of selection, but no account taken of results; following such preliminaries it would be possible to predict validity with some confidence. However, the ideal is rarely achieved. For example, consider how an aptitude test for computer programmers might be chosen. First, the work being done by the particular group of programmers would need to be studied; programmers work on different kinds of problems using different computer languages (software) and different computer equipment (hardware). Then, the information available about aptitude tests for computer programmers would need to be considered. If a test was to be a predictor of the performance of just one group of programmers (working on one type of problem using a single language and with one manufacturer's equipment designed three years ago) with what confidence can validity be assumed for other applications?

Other issues can also affect test validity, including the age, educational standard and test sophistication of the applicants. Accordingly, it is recommended that studies of the validity of the tests should always be carried out even if evidence of validity elsewhere is strong. The studies can be of three kinds.

Predictive validity is regarded as the best single measure of the worth of a test (see Chapter 1). However, there are very few people who have the technical expertise to carry out a proper study of predictive validity and there are a number of methodological and statistical pitfalls which can give misleading results to those who lack professional qualifications and expertise.

However, there are three reasons why those using tests should have some understanding of some of the steps involved in assessing validity. The first is that an understanding of some of the principles will help with the initial choice of tests and/or with the choice of expert advisers. The second is that it can be helpful for personnel managers and others to appreciate the kind of information that will need to be recorded and collated if validation studies are to be carried out. Third, it is important that personnel and other managers know how the worth of tests can be monitored so that they can seek expert advice if there are signs that all is not well.

Local studies which can be of some value are of two kinds:

(i)   subjective evaluation

(ii)   studies involving summarising data.

Advice on statistical analysis is also given.

Subjective evaluation

An initial form of validation that needs no statistical analysis, but which nevertheless has some worth, is to consider how the test results match up to observations. If an employee is tested, do the findings 'make sense' in terms of the experience of the person concerned? While the tests may point up some features or ideas about the individual that are new (if they did not, it would seem to have been fruitless asking for the tests to be done, unless for reassurance), the picture that emerges should not be unrecognisable. However, in view of 'the Barnum effect' (see Chapter 4) this is best regarded as an interim measure pending the collection of sufficient data for a proper validation study.

When evaluating test results by looking at the way a person behaves once they have been taken on, a danger to guard against is the self-fulfilling prophecy; in other words, people may see only what they expect to see. If the numbers to be followed-up are very small this may be the only kind of analysis that is feasible, but more rigorous approaches should be used if possible.

Studies which involve summarising data

Data that can be collected is essentially of three kinds:

- biographical data
- data about test scores
- data about job performance.

Biographical data need to be collected because one of the most important principles of summarising data is to compare 'like with like'. Test scores may depend on characteristics of those doing the tests (such as their age, sex, ethnic origin) while their job performance may depend on their length of service, education and many other factors other than test scores.

If numbers are small (less than 100) there is a danger that the sample may not be representative, and hence any trends must be viewed with caution. Sometimes numbers can be increased by 'pooling' data – for example, by combining the test scores of applicants at different sites or over several years, but it is best to take expert advice if 'pooling' is necessary.

If numbers are sufficient, look to see whether there appears to be a marked difference between, for example, the test scores of women under 20 and men over 45. If there are marked differences, keep the groups separate when doing further analysis (see below).

Data about test scores need to be collected to look at both the number of scores and their range. In order to check the worth of the test it is desirable that the actual test scores cover the full range of possible test scores and that, when drawn on a graph, the pattern of scores approximates to a bell-shaped curve called the normal curve (Figure 2). If selection decisions have taken the test scores into account there may be few, if any, low test scores among those taken on, and for this reason the curve may not be bell-shaped. To determine whether or not there is a full range and distribution of test scores look at the shape of the curve; also compare the scores of those recruited and those rejected and, in addition, the patterns of these scores compared with those for other groups reported in the test manual.

126

Figure 2

An illustration of the 'normal curve' using hypothetical test scores; each dot represents an individual obtaining the score.

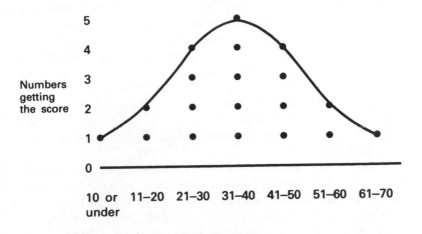

Test scores

Next, *data about job performance* need to be collected; the following are possibilities:

- ratings from managers or supervisors
- time to first promotion
- number of promotions gained
- salary growth
- tenure (length of stay)
- absences
- successful completion of training
- sales achieved by the individual.

Ideally, several of these measures should be used – otherwise there is a danger of the tests being selected on the basis of their ability to solve one problem (eg reducing the number of low performers being taken on) but at the expense of another (eg a rise in labour turnover).

127

As with test scores, it is important to look at the distribution of the data that have been collected. For example, it may be found that all those recruited are judged to be at least satisfactory and that few, if any, are judged less than satisfactory or unsatisfactory.

The final stage is to plot on to a series of graphs information combining test scores and job performance; if possible, each graph should comprise similar groups of people (eg females under 21) which are often referred to as sub-groups. These sub-groups can then be combined to form larger groups (eg all females).

Having drawn a series of graphs (or, if the numbers are small, just a single graph) the pattern of scores should be appraised; if the scores approximate to a line (straight, curved or even 'bow shaped') then use can be made of this pattern to predict job performance and the test is almost certainly valid.

If there is no pattern to the test scores, look back at the range of distributions of both the test scores and the measures of job performance. If the scores or measures do not cover a full range, the results may be inconclusive because, for example, it cannot be predicted how people with low scores would have performed if they had been recruited. Expert advice could then be sought on the application of statistical corrections.

If there is no pattern to the scores *and* there is a full range of test scores and measures of job performance there *may* be problems and it would be wise to seek advice from an occupational psychologist and/or the test supplier or publisher. However, remember that testing need be only a little bit better than chance to be commercially worthwhile and that marginal trends can be difficult to grasp visually. Also remember the rest of the selection process such as the interviews may not have been subject to the same scrutiny – do not assume that they would have been better if they were!

Statistical analyses

The summaries of data described in the previous section can go a long way to establishing whether a test is working. However, questions do arise that cannot be answered by summaries and graphs alone. For example:

- If part of the range of test scores is missing, can the 'true' validity of the test be estimated? (It can!)

- Which of two tests with similar graphical results is 'the best'?

- How can scores on different tests be combined together to give the most useful prediction?

- How do test scores compare with predictions from other ratings such as the assessments of interviewers?

Those with some statistical background will find guidance in books (eg Lewis, 1985; The Society for Industrial and Organisational Psychology, 1987) but as in other areas a little knowledge can be a dangerous thing; for example:

- Managers in one organisation compared test scores for apprentices with subsequent performance and, as a result, wrote an article claiming that tests supplied for apprentice selection were 'useless'; in fact, only those scoring in the top five per cent of marks had been recruited, but the lack of range of test scores had not been taken into account when validity had been assessed.

- A manager in another organisation suggested changing the design of a test on the basis of two samples of test scores each less than 30 in number; both samples came from the same office; the organisation was using 5,000 copies of the test annually spread over a number of locations!

Many different kinds of statistical analysis can be carried out on data from tests and assessments of performance. One common analysis is to determine whether or not the results are statistically significant. A statistically significant result is one that is unlikely to have occurred by chance, and there is a convention of using asterisks to indicate the level of confidence that can be placed in the results. The convention can be summarised thus:

* means that the probability of a result occurring by chance is less than 5 per cent (using statistical convention $p < 0.05$);

** means the probability of a chance result is less than 1 per cent ($p < 0.01$);

*** means the probability of a chance result is less than 0.1 per cent ($p < 0.001$).

When looking at the results of statistical analyses many factors must be taken into account, including the appropriateness of the statistics used. In particular, note that:

- small sample sizes make it less likely that statistically significant results will be found

- correlations may be of little practical value even if they are statistically significant; for example, correlations less than 0.10 would not normally be regarded as worthwhile for selection predictions

- correlations do not imply causation or explanations; for example, there *might* be a correlation between cups of tea drunk each day and take-home pay but people cannot increase their take-home pay by drinking more tea.

Accordingly, it is recommended that expert advice is taken from occupational psychologists who specialise in test validation (see Appendix 2). Their access to computing facilities will often speed up the calculations that need to be made.

Does the test discriminate fairly?

Effective tests discriminate on the basis of job-relevant characteristics. However, unfair discrimination should be avoided for a number of reasons. For example, it can be challenged on commercial grounds – if an organisation is precluding large numbers of potential applicants because of their sex, ethnic origin, etc, it may have difficulty in filling vacancies and surviving in the future. This would be critical for any British companies seeking US government contracts since such contracts are dependent on effective equal opportunities policies. In addition, it is important that any organisation aiming to provide a service to a wide cross-section of the community should be sensitive to a range of needs. Unfair discrimination can also be challenged because it is illegal and because suspicion of unfair discrimination can lead to costly enquiries; for example, industrial tribunals can be costly both in terms of meeting damages or other awards and in terms of the time the staff may need to prepare for the tribunal and to attend it. Further, there can be adverse public relations implications affecting both the perceived worth of top management and the attractiveness of the organisation to potential employees.

Checks should be made to ensure that tests are not discriminating unfairly against:

- members of one sex

- members of ethnic minority groups

- disabled people

- applicants of different ages.

Two kinds of check need to be made. The first is to see whether there are differences between sub-groups in terms of the range and distribution of the test scores. By way of example, assume that two clerical tests (A and B) are being tried out; the form of the trial is to administer both tests to all applicants but not to take the scores into account when making selection decisions.

At the end of the trial period a simple first analysis would involve computing summary tables of test scores for each test for each sub-group of interest; in Table 4, 50 male and 50 female candidates are being compared; both tests have a score range from 0 to 50. The distribution of scores achieved on Test A is the same for both men and women and at this stage the test does not discriminate unfairly against members of either sex. In contrast, women have done much better on Test B and, if a single cut-off point were to be used when selecting staff, unfair discrimination could be a problem; for example, if the cut-off point were to be 21, 23 men would be recruited and 37 women.

Table 4

| | Numbers achieving these scores | | | |
| | Test A | | Test B | |
Test Score	Male	Female	Male	Female
41–50	10	10	5	15
31–40	10	10	8	12
21–30	10	10	10	10
11–20	10	10	12	8
0–10	10	10	15	5

(NB   The range of scores achieved on a test will usually approximate to the normal curve shown in Figure 2 – Tables 4 and 5 have been simplified for the purposes of illustration).

There has been speculation about whether a second kind of discrimination might arise because the effectiveness of a test might vary from group to group, and this possibility should be checked too. The possibility is illustrated in the following example involving Test A only.

Imagine that six months after giving the test to the last of the applicants in the trial, the performance of the applicants is assessed and the relationship between test scores and job performance is tabulated; the results are shown in Table 5.

Table 5

Job performance

scores on test	Male and female combined		Male		Female	
	acceptable	*unacceptable*	*acceptable*	*unacceptable*	*acceptable*	*unacceptable*
A						
41–50	16	4	7	3	9	1
31–40	14	6	6	4	8	2
21–30	12	8	5	5	7	3
11–20	10	10	4	6	6	4
0–10	8	12	4	6	4	6

For Test A, Table 4 had shown no obvious unfair discrimination in the scores achieved by each sex. However, Table 5 shows a different predictive relationship between test score and job performance for men and women: a score of 11 or above indicates 60 per cent probability of acceptable job performance for women, while men need to achieve a score of 31 for the probability of acceptable job performance to be at the same level.

Thus while an overall pass mark of 21 would give a 60 per cent probability of acceptable job performance, this could be viewed as a discrimination against women whose chances of success would be 60 per cent with a score of only 11.

Thus, if a single cut-off is used, tests may discriminate unfairly against a particular sub-group because of differences in the overall distribution of test scores achieved and/or because of differences in the predictive relationship between test and job performance.

If findings of this kind arise in either case, the following issues need to be considered:

(i) First, have the numbers involved in analysis been large enough for statistically reliable conclusions to be drawn? Table 5 is based on 100 people but when divided into 20 'cells' some of the numbers are small and none are into double figures; this is one reason why total groups of 200 or more are desirable for statistical purposes.

(ii)   Second, could other factors be at play? Eg, in the case of clerical tests, male applicants may not have studied relevant subjects at school.

(iii)   Third, consider taking other action.

Each of these points will now be considered in turn.

Sample sizes

In order to draw accurate conclusions about the occurrence of unfair discrimination, there should ideally be at least 100 people in each of the sub-groups that are of interest. However, any gross differences may be apparent from samples half that size. While test users can often obtain adequate samples of male and female applicants, they can find it difficult to obtain sufficient numbers from different ethnic minority groups. (This raises the separate issue of how to categorise and group such individuals for this type of analysis – a complex issue in itself.)

If numbers are very small, they can sometimes be built up by reference to data collected about previous intakes of staff, to data collected about the same test by other employers, or to data collected by the test publisher. If a new and unproven test shows signs of unfair discrimination, results should not be taken into account at the time of selection and the validity of the test and the reasons for discrimination should be investigated expertly as soon as a sufficient sample has built up.

Circumstances

If differences in test performance are based on substantial sample sizes the underlying reasons should be investigated. It may be found, for example, that if previous experience (or lack of it) seems to be the reason for differences in performance some of the effects of previous experience might be overcome by offering relevant experience prior to testing (eg a special short course).

Taking other action

The following possibilities should be considered and expert advice taken on them:

●   Can an alternative test be found which is equally effective in terms of predictive validity but which does not discriminate?

- Can the test be redesigned so that those items that are discriminating unfairly are dropped?

- Can alternative tests (or even alternative methods of selection) be offered to applicants? For example, potential applicants could be sifted either by passing public or internal examinations, or by passing an aptitude test, or by attending a job-related training course.

If none of the above possibilities is feasible, the apparent conflict between the spirit and the letter of the law presents real problems for responsible employers wishing to comply with current legislation. The dilemma is illustrated by the following example. Suppose that for several years tests have been administered to 2,000 applicants (1,000 male and 1,000 female) in order to shortlist 100 for interview, and that the same pass mark has been used for both groups. Follow-up shows that this has resulted in 70 males being called for interview and 30 females, ie 7 per cent of males and 3 per cent of females. Follow-up also shows that the test has been an effective predictor of performance, so there is reluctance to consider any of the alternatives described above.

Under these circumstances an employer wishing to observe the spirit of the law might continue to shortlist the 7 per cent of males but to increase the number of females shortlisted to 7 per cent as well. This would increase the numbers that are shortlisted but would avoid the challenge that males are being disadvantaged (7 per cent would still be called for shortlisting) or that females were the subject of discrimination (the percentage called forward would now be identical to that for the men).

While such a strategy might satisfy the spirit of the law its operation in the example given would depend on the use of lower 'pass' marks for women. This would appear to conflict with the current legislation which requires that all candidates taking the same procedure are treated equally.

Where such conflicts are apparent in legislation it is normal for them to be resolved by either the hearing of a test case so that law can be established or by revision of the legislation.

The same principles can be followed when scrutinising for fairness among ethnic minority groups and disabled people. Remember that in order to be able to check the fairness of the tests (and the whole selection procedure) in this way, appropriate details must be collected from applicants at the time of selection.

Scrutiny for fairness should not be confined to tests. In particular, make sure that interviewers have received appropriate training and monitor their assessments with the same rigour as for test scores; Professor Robert Guion has drawn attention to the need to check the fairness not only of the selection methods but also the decision-making process and the individual decision makers.

Readers who wish to go into this very complex area are recommended to obtain a booklet entitled *Discriminating Fairly: A Guide to Fair Selection* which was published jointly by The British Psychological Society and the Runnymede Trust, or one of the other specialist publications in this area (eg Pearn, 1979).

Benefits, costs and potential problems

These are considered under the following headings:

- the potential benefits of testing to the employing organisation
- the costs of testing to the employing organisation
- other risks and possible costs
- utility analysis.

Potential benefits of testing to the employing organisation

The essential benefits of testing to the employing organisation can be considered under two broad headings: financial benefits and other benefits.

Financial benefits

The use of tests can lead to substantial financial benefits for two reasons:

(a) the quality of selection and hence the productivity of employees may be improved; further, there may be other benefits such as improved quality of work, reduced turnover etc;

(b) the cost of processing large numbers of applications can be minimised.

(a) Improving the quality of selection: Tests can provide measurements of qualities which it may be difficult or impossible to assess at selection by any other means. Examples range from aptitude for computer programming to dexterity for particular tasks. The correct use of tests can therefore allow the organisation to make a better match

135

between an individual and a job. The use of tests can thus contribute to the cost effectiveness of selection in three ways. First, because the job performance of those taken on may prove to be better than if tests were not used. Second, because those selected by the improved methods may need less training and stay longer, thus reducing an organisation's recruitment and training bills. Third, because those taken on may be more suitable than external applicants when it comes to promotion to a higher level and hence the cost of subsequent recruitment may also be reduced. However, the needs of subsequent jobs will have to be taken into account at the time of selection if this third benefit is to be achieved.

In a job where performance can be measured objectively, it is possible to calculate the actual financial savings that can be achieved by improving selection and thus increasing output or reducing the numbers of employees required to meet the output targets. (Schmidt and Hunter, 1979; Hunter and Schmidt, 1982; Smith, 1986). In a paper describing assessment centres (including psychometric tests) used in the selection of senior police and prison officers, Bedford and Feltham (1986) estimated annual net savings of over £1.3 million.

For many management jobs it is not possible to quantify the actual savings in this way, but the financial benefit to be gained by an organisation from making a good selection decision is potentially far greater. In many cases it may not be only the salary and overheads associated with employing the individual that are at stake, but the future prospects of the company if a bad decision is made.

(b) Minimising the cost of processing large numbers of applications: Mention has already been made of the use of tests as a way of 'sifting' applications; the aim of sifting is to increase the final selection ratio (see Chapter 5).

Other potential benefits of testing

Monitoring and maintenance of standards: The use of tests allows comparison between applicants both over time and at different places. Tests can therefore help in the maintenance of selection standards from year to year among areas and regions both within and outside an organisation. Most commercially available tests have a wide range of norms available which allow comparisons to be made with similar applications to other organisations, although such data are normally supplied in confidence by the users to the test publishers and the names of the supplying organisations may not be known to other users. Large organisations may have enough data to draw up their own comparative norms as well. The standard of individual applicants can be compared and one applicant group can be judged against another. Without tests, it is more difficult to make objective comparisons and it is likely to be some time before variations in the standard of applicants, and thus possibly of recruits, become evident – possibly to the cost of the employing organisation.

Attracting better applicants: Some organisations believe that the use of tests helps to attract better applicants. This was certainly the case when War Office Selection Boards for officer selection replaced recommendations made by commanding officers after 15-minute interviews (Toplis and Stewart, 1983). More recently, graduate applicants indicated that they chose a particular organisation because they were impressed by the opportunities they were given to show the skills and abilities they had. (They often have little else to go on.) The more systematic and professional the selection procedure, the more likely it is to be perceived by the candidate as fair and effective. (Rynes *et al*, 1980).

Encouraging self-selection: Some tests convey information to the candidate about the nature and content of the job for which they have applied, thus encouraging self-selection and increasing the likelihood of the organisation getting the best person for the job.

Improving candidates' self-perception: The very process of taking tests may help candidates to improve their self-perception and thus contribute to their being able to make a better choice of career and organisation, whether or not they are offered or take the particular job for which they have applied. If tests are used widely, this could provide a broader benefit to all organisations by leading to a better match between individuals and jobs.

Costs of testing to the employing organisation
Against the expected financial and other benefits, the potential user must set the cost of gaining access to testing expertise and introducing and sustaining a testing programme. Here the main issues in terms of costs are summarised.

Gaining access to testing expertise
Ways of gaining access to testing expertise, and the costs involved, were described in Chapter 4.

Introducing and sustaining a testing programme
Once testing expertise is available there are four main stages in introducing and sustaining a testing programme; first, training test administrators, second, obtaining the materials, third, monitoring the programme and fourth, reviewing the programme. The costs likely to be incurred at each of these stages are as follows:

(a) *Training accredited testers:* Training often involves residential training courses. Costs are incurred both for the registration and residential fees, and also as a result of absence from work. In 1997, the cost of one week's residential training was up to £1,920 excluding VAT and a person wishing to use a full range of tests from one supplier would pay £4,000 in residential training fees alone. Because courses differ in the tests offered, training venues etc, there can be marked differences in fees charged.

(b) *Obtaining test materials:* Such a range and diversity of psychological tests are available that it is impossible to give any idea of typical costs. However, in 1997 some question booklets cost around £19 to lease for a year and some answer sheets around £5. Catalogues and price lists are produced annually by most suppliers; current price lists should be checked by organisations that are calculating the costs of introducing testing. At least one publisher also charges licensing fees which, in 1997, were up to £1,450 per test for a corporate licence fee. Although costs can be substantial, these are minor compared with the costs incurred if, for example, errors are made in the appointment of senior managers whose influence may extend well beyond their own department.

(c) *Monitoring a testing programme:* Once a testing system is established, organisations need to allocate resources for monitoring tests to make sure they are being used properly; without such monitoring it is possible that some of those administering tests may fall into bad habits – it is surprising how many test administrators are tempted to alter the time allowed for tests, etc. 'Monitoring' can also involve making sure that managers do not start to develop their own tests – some are tempted to do so because they do not realise the ways in which a test should be developed, constructed and normed, nor do they appreciate the rigours of administration and scoring, the use of norms for assessment, the possibility of unfair discrimination, and so on.

(d) *Reviewing a testing programme:* Jobs often evolve over time and the relationship between a particular test and job performance may therefore have changed. Educational and employment opportunities may also affect the numbers and quality of applicants coming forward. Accordingly, the validity of every test should be checked at regular intervals (eg every five years, and more frequently if there are distinct changes in all or any of these areas).

138

Other risks and possible costs

The main areas where costs will be incurred have now been described. However, there are also other, non-financial, risks accompanying testing which an organisation should be aware of, and consider. These are obtaining effective tests, test security, test popularity, possible adverse effects on candidates, possible outside scrutiny, registration under the Data Protection Act.

Obtaining effective tests

Selecting the right test for the right situation is not always easy. Ghiselli (1966) examined the results of many studies which had been conducted on the validity of tests in the selection and placement of workers in a wide range of occupations and found large variations in validity. Several ideas have been put forward as to why such variations may be occurring, including the possibility of inappropriate tests being used.

Another possible pitfall is the unsuccessful transfer of the use of a test or tests which have been successful in selecting applicants in one situation. Even jobs with identical titles may have differences which affect the ability of the test to predict job success and the differences may not be apparent if only superficial enquiries are made. For example, there may be differences in the level of responsibility and decisions to be made, in the type of figure work to be done, in the equipment to be used, in the way the work is supervised, in the noise, heating or other environmental conditions, and so on.

Test security

From time to time there are reports of tests being compromised. For example, one company found its manual dexterity test – involving placing washers and nuts on to screw threads – had been studiously copied and that some applicants were attending for practice at a nearby house before going on to the company for their proper test. While there is nothing wrong with practice sessions *per se*, and indeed many tests have a built-in supervised practice session, it is important in selection to treat all applicants equally; either all applicants should have opportunities to practice for the specified and carefully timed period or no one should.

Accordingly, every effort *must* be made to maintain test security (eg applicants should not have the opportunity to copy the test materials) and if tests are heavily used parallel forms should be professionally developed so that applicants are unlikely to know the particular version that they are given.

139

Test popularity

The popularity of some commercially available tests can lead to further difficulties. For example, in graduate recruitment it is possible that the same applicant will take the same tests in several different organisations within a relatively short period, since there are relatively few different tests available for graduate recruitment in the UK. In general this is likely to result in some applicants steadily improving their scores as they remember some 'correct' answers and thus have more time to work out answers to other questions, but exceptions have been noted. It is important to establish whether or not previous experience of the tests is affecting results – if test scores are enhanced by prior experience, unsuitable candidates may be 'passed', while if prior experience depresses scores, suitable candidates may be rejected.

It is also important to consider the possibility that some applicants might have distorted their responses to psychometric questionnaires in an attempt to 'improve' the profile that they obtained on a previous occasion.

Possible adverse effects on candidates

A potential problem in the use of tests is that some applicants may lack confidence in their own abilities and not put themselves forward if testing is involved. The possibility of intimidation is a particular problem when dealing with less academic school-leavers, disabled candidates, older candidates, people trying to return to work after a period of non-employment, etc. However, in order to try to overcome this problem and minimise any advantage or disadvantage to particular groups which could arise from their 'ability to take tests', many tests have example questions for candidates to do in their own time, before starting the test proper; the example questions enable the candidates to familiarise themselves with the format of the questions and reduce their fears. Another way to deal with this is to provide applicants with a handout explaining, in friendly non-technical language, why tests are being used and giving example questions (see Chapter 7). The use of computers and/or recorded instructions may also help to minimise any fears (see Chapter 12).

Possible outside scrutiny

Organisations that use tests may have to justify their actions to bodies such as the Equal Opportunities Commission (EOC) or the Commission for Racial Equality (CRE) and appropriate analyses were described earlier in this chapter. The EOC and CRE may wish to look into the origins and worth of a test if a complaint about its fairness is made. However, there is no reason to think that either the EOC or CRE will look at a test any more than they look at any other aspect of selection procedures, including application forms and interviews. If the content of the test has been carefully matched to the requirements of the job and its use is based on past experience of the reasons for success and failure (as it should be), it is very unlikely that either body will find any reason to investigate. Nevertheless, care should be taken that tests avoid the use of colloquial English, and do not assume knowledge more likely to be known by one sex than the other, one racial group than another, etc.

Registration under the Data Protection Act, 1984
If test scores linked to individuals' names are to be kept on computer, it is necessary that the employing organisation registers this under the terms of the Data Protection Act. If an organisation's computer system is already registered under the Act, it should be only an administrative formality to add an extra item (ie test scores) to the specification. However, once individuals are granted rights of access to personal details that are held on computer, organisations whose systems include test scores will have to develop procedures for providing individuals with meaningful feedback about their performance and take appropriate steps regarding copyright (see Chapter 5); raw scores alone are at best meaningless and at worst dangerous and open to misinterpretation (see Chapters 8 and 12).

Test results should not stay on the computer after their useful life unless they are to form part of a validation or other study (see Chapter 8). Also, steps must be taken to ensure that only accredited users have access to this information.

Utility analysis
Utility analysis is the technical name for a type of cost-benefit analysis which enables the monetary value of selection procedures – or, indeed, anything else that affects the quality of human resources, such as a training programme – to be calculated. Utility analysis can be used to establish the worth of introducing or changing selection tests. In Appendix 8, Jeannette James explains how to carry out such an analysis.

Summary

This chapter has described three possible ways of establishing the worth of tests, and how checks can be made as to whether or not the tests are discriminating fairly.

The benefits, costs and potential problems involved in testing have been drawn together under the following headings:

- the potential benefits
- the main potential costs
- other risks and possible costs
- utility analysis.

11
Testing in a Wider Context: Other methods of assessment and development

Nowadays a growing number of methods other than psychometrics are used to assess and develop people's ability, aptitude, personality and motivation. These methods include psychometric instruments as an important input to the process, for example assessment or development centres (already referred to briefly in Chapter 2), self-development workshops, 360-degree appraisals and team-development workshops. At the heart of most of these you will find the competencies approach to identifying and assessing personal characteristics. In this chapter we shall describe the competencies approach, the most common alternative methods, the role of tests within them, and their relative advantages and disadvantages.

Competency models

The competency approach was devised in the 1970s by the US consultancy company McBer, to identify those personal characteristics which result in effective or superior performance in a job. According to Boyatzis (1982), in his book that documents the McBer work, 'a job competency is an underlying characteristic of a person in that it may be a motive, trait, skill, aspect of one's self-image or social role, or a body of knowledge which he or she uses'. He also introduces the important concept of the 'threshold' competency: those characteristics just mentioned that are essential to performing the job but are not causally related to superior performance. Competencies were identified using interviews incorporating the critical incident technique. However, according to Boyatzis, his study 'does not provide enough information for the development or implementation of selection or promotion systems'. This approach is often referred to as personal competencies, as opposed to the occupational competencies or standards approach adopted in the UK since the late 1980s. The latter concentrates on the job, as opposed to the individual, and aims to specify in very detailed behavioural terms the standards of performance required to carry out a job competently or effectively. The standards approach is used widely in the UK as an assessment tool for accrediting National Vocational Qualifications (NVQs) for a wide range of jobs from semi-skilled up to middle-management levels. The Management Charter Initiative (MCI) has produced standards for first level, middle and senior management levels. However, in this chapter we shall concentrate on the personal competencies approach, because it focuses on the individual's personal characteristics, and so is much more appropriate to assessment and development applications.

One of the first personal competency models developed in the UK was the job competencies survey, now called the personal competencies survey (PCS), which has evolved over the last 20 years through the work of Dulewicz (1997) in the fields of assessment centres (ACs) and management competencies. The first version, produced in 1986, drew heavily on the literature at the time and was originally used as a questionnaire for the first stage of the job analysis process for identifying competencies of senior and middle managers in large companies such as Shell International, Barclays, British Gas and Smiths Industries. It was first used for appraisal in 1988 on the executive development workshop within the general and senior management courses at Henley Management College, and has just been revised after eight years of extensive applications and research in many countries.

The overall framework is very comprehensive, consisting as it now does of 45 competencies under six main headings covering intellectual, personal, communication, interpersonal, leadership and results-orientation competencies. (For more details of the specific competencies, see Table 6.) The behavioural definitions of the competencies, and information on the 360-degree appraisal procedure for which it is used, appear in Dulewicz (1997). This model is fairly typical of the generic competency frameworks currently used in the UK.

Assessment and development centres

The assessment centre method of identifying potential is primarily a British invention, formulated in World War II by the Armed Forces in the form of the War Office Selection Board, and followed soon after by the Civil Service. The first industrial application, however, was in the USA by the telephone company AT&T in 1955, and since then its use

Table 6: Personal Competencies Framework

I Intellectual

1. Information collection
2. Problem analysis
3. Numerical interpretation
4. Judgement
5. Critical faculty
6. Creativity
7. Planning
8. Perspective
9. Organisational awareness
10. External awareness
11. Learning-oriented
12. Technical expertise

II Personal

13. Adaptability
14. Independence
15. Integrity
16. Stress tolerance
17. Resilience
18. Detail consciousness
19. Self-management
20. Change-oriented

III Communication

21. Reading
22. Written communication
23. Listening
24. Oral expression
25. Oral presentation

IV Interpersonal

26. Impact
27. Persuasiveness
28. Sensitivity
29. Flexibility
30. Ascendancy
31. Negotiating

V Leadership

32. Organising
33. Empowering
34. Appraising
35. Motivating others
36. Developing others
37. Leading

VI Results-orientation

38. Risk-taking
39. Decisiveness
40. Business sense
41. Energy
42. Concern for excellence
43. Tenacity
44. Initiative
45. Customer-oriented

has mushroomed to the point that the latest estimates suggest there are about 3000 centres in that country alone. The picture in the UK is very similar – more than a half of medium-sized and large companies use assessment centre (AC) exercises, according to recent surveys.

An AC is a multifaceted, multidimensional approach in which a number of personal characteristics or personal competencies (see above) required for successful performance at the target level or job are first identified and then assessed, using a range of situational exercises designed to simulate tasks at the target level, psychometric ability tests and personality questionnaires. The exercises are normally observed and assessed by a team of assessors specially trained for the task of systematic assessment, who make evaluations and make recommendations for potential and action plans.

A typical AC will include some or all of the following exercises:

- an *in-tray (in-basket)* exercise which usually contains 20-35 items, nearly all of which should be based on actual items from target job holders' in-trays, although a few can be specially designed to tie together the other items in the fictitious company on which the exercise is based. It normally takes up to two hours, and is followed by an interview with one of the assessors who probes the actions taken on high-priority items and also the general approach adopted.

- a *leaderless group discussion* in which four to six participants normally form a committee to achieve a given objective. Often an individual is asked to support a particular course of action, and to convince his or her peers of the merits of their case.

- an *assigned leader exercise*, in which participants take turns to be the leader for a specific period. A different topic or task is presented to each member of the group to tackle.

- a *presentation* on a particular topic of relevance to the target job. The participants present their case individually, to one or two of the assessors. Typically they will each have about 10 minutes for their presentation, followed by up to 10 minutes of probing questions from the assessors.

- a *written report* , also on a subject of relevance to the target job. The participants are usually asked to write a three- or four-page report.

- a *role-play exercise* in which the participant is typically asked to conduct a fact-finding, sales or disciplinary interview with a subordinate or customer, played by a trained member of staff.

In many centres it is common for ability tests and personality questionnaires to be administered as well. Cognitive (often verbal and numerical critical thinking) tests normally relate solely to the competence 'analysis', whereas personality questionnaire results will apply to a number of the interpersonal, motivational and emotional adjustment competencies. Often, personality results are fed into the assessors' conference by a psychologist or accredited tester whenever they appear relevant to the discussion.

One reason why ACs are so widely used is because of problems found with alternative methods, such as appraisal systems or committees of wise managers. These often arise when the demands of more senior positions are significantly different from those of the current job; the competencies required are likely to be very different, so one cannot expect current performance to be an accurate guide to future potential. Psychological tests can be a valuable measure of a person's intellectual capacities, personality and motivation, but they do not always provide a comprehensive assessment of all the relevant competencies or the degree of behavioural detail often required to identify a full enough set of training and development needs. There are two other main reasons for this trend. First, the scientific evidence: even a small increase in validity can result in a disproportionately large increase in the net benefit derived, in performance and monetary value of staff selected. Second, numerous case-studies from a range of different organisations have been published in recent years to testify to the great benefit derived by both participants and assessors from taking part in an AC, and the evidence from the vast majority of more than 50 validation studies in a meta-analysis indicates that ACs predict future performance or success very well, certainly better than any other widely researched assessment tool (Gaugler, Rosenthal, Thornton and Bentson, 1987).

For many years, ACs focused largely or exclusively on the assessment of potential for the next job up, or on longer-term prospects over the next five years or so. These events were run primarily for the benefit of the organisations, with the participant gaining little or no feedback, apart from whether he or she got the job. However, over the last decade or two, the aims of many centres have switched, with much greater emphasis being placed on the development of participants. Many centres nowadays combine assessment of potential with detailed feedback to participants, who will have a lengthy feedback session with an assessor, culminating in an agreed action plan to help him or her to address those weaknesses identified in the centre that are relevant to realising his or her full potential. Some centres are now run purely for the benefit of the participant, who 'owns' all the data collected. Assessors, usually called observers or facilitators, provide evaluations of performance to participants and advise on interpretation and action planning. But it is the individual who is responsible for collating and interpreting the information, and for organising the follow-up action.

Whereas in the USA it is the norm not to use psychometric tests and questionnaires in ACs or development centres, in the UK they are usually incorporated, and in many events they play a central role. They add invaluable information in two main ways. First, they provide a rigorous, objective assessment of mental ability and ultimate capacity of participants that cannot always be spotted by assessors. It can be extremely valuable to know that a participant who has performed poorly in some exercises has in fact got a high level of mental ability. Such information will usually stimulate a valuable debate in the assessor's conference. Second, with personality data, it is sometimes very difficult for assessors to evaluate accurately some competencies, especially those in the emotional or motivation domains, even in a two-day event. Internal states can be assessed much more accurately and objectively by personality questionnaires, even if the data are based on self-perceptions. Once again, any differences can be fruitfully explored in the assessor's conference. So, unlike the USA, where the ACs are usually seen as an alternative approach to psychometrics, tests in the UK are normally used to provide evidence that complements the assessor's judgement, and which can be particularly valuable in its own right in development centres.

An extensive literature exists for those who wish to study the subject in more detail. Thornton and Byham (1982) and Woodruffe (1990) provide very comprehensive overviews. For details of setting up and running ACs, and for relating them to competency frameworks, see Dulewicz (1989; 1991).

Self- and team-development workshops

Self-development workshops are often used as an alternative to an AC, and have been described as 'ACs without the situational exercises'. They depend heavily on psychometric and other instruments which are usually completed by participants, their bosses, their subordinates and other staff. This approach is currently called 360-degree appraisal (see below). Self-development workshops normally address not only competencies but also personality, leadership style, stress, attitudes, career anchors and aspirations, and motivation. The workshop leader often provides a theoretical input on these matters, and will then guide participants through the interpretation of their scores. Sharing results and discussion amongst participants is also usually encouraged. The result is an action plan which members pursue back on the job, often under the guidance of a mentor.

Team-building workshops are a variant of self-development workshops, in which established or new teams are assembled in order to develop their group process and working procedures. Teams usually work under the guidance of a facilitator who instructs them on the nature of group process and working procedures, and shows them how to develop their own methods, tailored to the needs of their team, and how to improve team performance. Both practical and cerebral exercises are the main vehicles used, but personality questionnaires often provide an invaluable input, since questionnaires such as 16PF and OPQ® produce 'second-order' factor scores on highly relevant constructs such as team roles, leadership style and follower style. Such data can be invaluable for informing members about the composition of the team, for helping teams to understand why they are performing below their best, and sometimes for giving an indication of how a member might develop both as an individual and as a team member.

360-degree appraisal

In contrast to ACs and development workshops in which, as just noted, psychometrics have an important role, the 360-degree appraisal approach is used nowadays by many organisations as an alternative to ability and personality testing. In this section we provide an overview of the process, and use as an example one of the first systems to be developed in the UK (Dulewicz, 1997).

Questionnaires have been used as a vital tool in appraisal and job analysis for over 50 years, but there has been a major growth in their use in recent years. In appraisal, the emphasis has traditionally been on the annual review by the boss, with the results determining pay increases. Research has shown, however, that this process has done little for the development of staff and often sets the wrong climate for this. Therefore other processes have evolved to achieve this end. There has also been a change in the focus of appraisal, and the factors under review, with the dramatic growth in the use of competencies since the early 1980s when, as just mentioned, the US consultancy McBer first pioneered this approach. In addition, with recent trends towards flatter organisations, teamworking and greater openness and involvement, we have seen a shift away from solo appraisal by the boss, towards multiple appraisal by all who have contact with the employee, even subordinates and customers. To capture the flavour of this all-round view, the process has become known as 360-degree appraisal.

A 360-degree appraisal process gathers ratings of participants' current performance on each competence from themselves and from other people who know them well, against the standards expected at their level in the organisation. These 'self' and 'other' ratings of current proficiency provide views from different vantage points. These views may not all be exactly the same because the other people will probably have seen participants working in different situations, and so have seen different facets of their performance. There is also inevitably a degree of subjectivity in these ratings. Notwithstanding, these views provide a detailed and comprehensive picture of current performance, and participants are encouraged to stand back and identify the true picture which should emerge.

All the information gathered about the present and future importance of the various competencies, and the ratings of performance are usually brought together in a report. A typical report would cover:

- definitions of the competencies appraised

- the competencies that are important

- a summary and overview of performance

- detailed analysis of performance, covering strengths, development needs, growth needs, and under-utilised potential

- action planning.

In their report, participants are normally encouraged to draw up action plans to enable them to maximise their learning opportunities. Participants are often advised to find a 'facilitator' – an individual with great experience of personal development – to help with this difficult but important task. Inputs on key issues relating to human abilities, personality, motivation, attitudes and other relevant subjects should also be sought from their facilitator to help with the action-planning.

Relative advantages and disadvantages

Tests have been the most widely used scientific assessment tool for the last 75 years. As we have seen above, this is largely because:

- they are derived from well-researched models in the scientific literature

- the constructs measured are clearly defined

- results are standardised and hence objective

- users must be well-trained and accredited

- validation studies have demonstrated their value for predicting future performance.

Rigour and validity are the main reasons why tests are used, both in isolation and as an important and integral part of other methods just described. Their main disadvantages appear to be that:

- they are based almost exclusively on self-report, although one personality questionnaire has recently included for the first time a version which allows rating by others – this may be the start of a trend.

- they do not provide the degree of detailed, relevant and comprehensive behavioural data generated by ACs and by 360-degree appraisals. This type of output can be valuable when drawing up action plans from these methods.

- they must be administered by qualified users and materials are restricted – they cannot, for example, be sent out by post. Unfortunately, these positive features can add significantly to the cost, and so to the attractiveness of some other methods.

- while the validity of ability tests is almost universally accepted, doubts still linger in some quarters about personality questionnaires because of a few articles, some highly misleading, in the press a few years ago.

Many users find other methods attractive because of these disadvantages of tests. The validity of ACs is, however, even higher than for tests, or any other single method, primarily because it gets the best of all worlds by incorporating several different methods, including tests. Most self- and team-development workshops are only as valid as the tests used within them. And the case for 360-degree appraisal, in terms of its scientific properties, has yet to be fully established. It has many positive features, especially its comprehensiveness in terms of the use of multiple raters, and the wide range of relevant competencies able to be assessed, but there is a long way to go before the method can compete on scientific grounds with the vast literature on testing that goes back 75 years.

Summary

Psychometric tests do not measure performance and behaviour at work; rather, the results of testing are a source of predictions and of explanations which can play an important part in selection and development decisions.

Accordingly, test results have to be considered alongside information from other methods of assessment and development. While these other methods also vary in their accuracy and rigour, they have a part to play in making the best possible decisions about and with people.

12
Current developments and keeping informed

Developments have moved on apace since the second edition of this book was published in 1991. The trends we identified then have largely continued, though not all to the same extent. Before considering the present picture it is perhaps worth reviewing those earlier trends to see where they have got to today. There were five trends:

- adopting a more organised and ethical approach to testing

- a considerable increase in the use of advanced selection methods

- the growing use of computers in testing

- government legislation

- the role of The British Psychological Society in promoting higher standards in test use.

Adopting a more organised and ethical approach to testing

In the past, it was common for psychometric testing and assessment practices to develop in a fairly random, almost haphazard, fashion in response to organisational needs as they arose. This often led to rather anomalous situations in which individuals who were being assessed for different levels of management or for widely differing jobs found themselves taking the same battery of tests – which they understandably found more than a little odd. Another example was to find various business units of a given organisation using completely different tests and test norms for recruitment to what were, to all intents and purposes, exactly the same roles. The result was a lack of standardisation that led to increased costs and a reduced transferability of information.

In the late 1980s and early 1990s some companies progressed beyond this stage and began to develop a more strategic approach to assessment, integrating their activities in this field into a more coherent policy that was properly bedded into HR practices. A good example of this in ICL was described by Jones (1990). To some extent this has continued, though perhaps not as far as it might. Where progress has been made, it is mostly within the context of identifying key competencies within an organisation, and then using these as a common framework and language for guiding selection, performance management and career development processes. This has certainly helped to make testing practices more consistent in the way that they are applied. However, over the last five or six years the tendency to devolve responsibility to line business units rather than to determine policy from the centre has continued in many organisations, with the result that it is not uncommon to find different business units using different tests (and, more to the point, tests of differing levels of difficulty) for much the same jobs.

As far as ethical use of tests is concerned, the efforts of The BPS and the IPD have had some effect, as have a number of industrial tribunal cases (see Pickard, 1996). There has been increased sensitivity to candidates' perception of their treatment in selection, particularly in relation to test-taking. Barclays Bank's psychometric testing and assessment centre policy document is still probably the outstanding example of how an organisation can try to ensure that test use is both ethical and effective while still allowing individual business units reasonable freedom to determine the best assessment tools to meet their local needs. Unfortunately, very few other companies have given the same amount of time, resources and thought to this, and there has been less progress here in the last few years than one might have hoped.

The increased use of advanced selection methods

Although the UK went through a major recession in the early 1990s, there has been little sign of it in the field of psychometric testing. Not only do all the surveys show that test use has increased, but the actual product range has widened significantly; there is a seemingly never-ending stream of new psychological tests coming on to the market. The same pattern is visible in much of the rest of Europe, though perhaps a year or two behind the UK position. More recently, the rate of growth seems to have slowed a little; to some extent, this is perhaps inevitable, but it is also owing to concerns over possible legal challenges to test use, as mentioned previously. One other factor is the growth in popularity of so-called 360-degree feedback systems mentioned earlier in this book (see Chapter 11); in a developmental context, these are sometimes seen as alternatives to psychometric tests, though in reality they produce a different kind of information.

Despite this slight tailing-off of the growth curve, personality measures seem to be used by about 65-70 per cent of the major employing organisations, the equivalent figures for cognitive tests and assessment or development centres being 70-75 per cent and 55-60 per cent respectively.

Growth of computer use in testing

Computer technology continues to influence testing by providing new methods of administering, scoring, interpreting and monitoring testing. It is also providing new ways of testing and of test development. Each area of innovation is separate but now that access to computer equipment is available changes are likely to take place in several areas. Readers should note that the laws of copyright apply and that placing a test or associated information (such as answers or norms) on a computer without the publisher's agreement constitutes infringement of copyright.

Each area of innovation is now discussed in turn, detailing first the potential benefits and then the possible disadvantages.

Test administration

The use of small business and other computers offer many potential advantages (French, 1986) over tests in a pencil-and-paper form. For example:

- A wider variety of test content can be used (particularly those involving perceptual tasks and response times).

- The facility for 'adaptive' or 'tailored' testing becomes available; adaptive testing means those taking the test can, on the basis of the speed and correctness of response, be moved through the test to those items for which their chances of success are close to 50 per cent; the test is completed when a sample of these items has been attempted and thus the time required for testing can be considerably shortened; in turn, this shortened time can help to make the testing procedure more acceptable to the candidates.

- The distribution of test material may be simplified if testing continues to be carried out at several locations. Instead of sending out question booklets, answer sheets etc, it may be sufficient to send out small floppy discs which can then be used over and over again until such time as the test is revised. Because of the small size of the floppy disks the cost of registered postage and other charges are likely to be considerably lower, while the security of the tests is likely to be as high if not higher.

- A high level of standardisation can be achieved in the administration of tests by computer; computer-administered tests can be virtually self-administering – the role of the administrator can be to check the applicant's name, to sit him or her in front of the keyboard and screen, and to tell the applicant what to do if help is required, or if there is a problem with the equipment, etc. After this very brief person-to-person contact the applicant can be left to read the instructions on the computer screen and comprehension can be checked by appropriate questions; in particular, the timing of the tests can be carried out by the computer equipment, avoiding problems due to the lack of a stopwatch or a similarly accurate timer, inaccurate timing arising from human error, and even a wish by the test administrator to alter the times allowed to increase the chances of success. The motives for altering times range from empathy with the candidates (or lack of it) through to the need to fill vacancies, or even the fact that recruiters are sometimes paid bonuses according to the number of staff they take on and therefore want to get as many through the test as possible.

- The use of computers and the range of techniques that they offer for both presenting questions and collecting replies can help in the assessment of handicapped and disabled people.

- A number of studies have been carried out to see whether applicants prefer computer-administered tests to those administered in other ways; unfortunately, some of these studies have been based on an unsatisfactory experimental design, eg one study involved asking people who had taken the computer-administered test whether they preferred it to the pencil-and-paper version, but without having the pencil-and-paper version available for inspection. While studies have so far failed to identify any group of applicants for whom the computer-administered test was not the preferred choice, there remains concern that some groups (eg older people) may find the different presentation off-putting.

- Once available, computers can help in organising the testing programme, eg by producing letters to be sent to candidates, programmes for interviewers, etc.

It is clear that there are many advantages to computer administration. The disadvantages are as follows:

- The lack of personal contact and interest that a test administrator can give may mean that some candidates lose interest.

- The test has to be designed (or redesigned) for computer administration. If a computerised version of a test does not exist, programming expertise will be involved; also it must not be assumed that results from a pencil-and-paper test and a version of the test which is computer-administered are directly comparable because, for example, there may not be the same opportunity for the candidate to ask questions of the administrators. Even if changes have been kept to a minimum the effect of relatively subtle changes may be important. For example, on a pencil-and-paper test, candidates may mark questions about which they are uncertain and return to them after they have attempted all the other items; the facility to mark and go back to questions in a computerised version of the test may not be available. Accordingly different norms and cut-offs may have to be developed and used according to whether candidates have taken the pencil-and-paper or computerised versions of a test.

- The initial finance required for computerised testing can be high, particularly if large groups of candidates need to be tested at the same time and large numbers of computers or terminals are therefore required. In theory it might be possible to offset the cost by using the equipment for other purposes; thus, a group of six terminals might be used for training in computing or other subjects when not required for testing; costs may also be kept down by making use of existing terminals or other computer equipment but in practice:

  ○ the equipment may not be free to be used for testing

  ○ the equipment may not be suitable from a technical point of view (eg, the computer language may be inappropriate, the computer memory may be too small, etc)

  ○ the location of the equipment may make it unsuitable for testing, eg a number of terminals may exist but be located on the desks of key staff in a number of busy offices with telephone and other background noises; thus the environment may be totally unsuitable for testing

  ○ a fourth problem with computerised administration concerns the storage of responses. Under the Data Protection Act, individuals are entitled to a copy of the information stored about them on computer. To protect copyright, they may be denied access to any records of their replies to individual questions, but once the replies have been scored it would seem appropriate to allow access to at least the total scores on tests or sub-tests; precisely what applicants can demand will, no doubt, be established by test cases in the courts of law.

○ finally, it is possible that the results of adaptive or tailored testing could also be challenged legally because applicants are not being given identical tests; such a challenge is considered unlikely in the USA because of the familiarity of the judges, prosecutors and defendants with the principle of test design and with the *Standards for Educational and Psychological Testing*, recently published by three eminent US organisations including the American Psychological Association (1985). It remains to be seen whether adaptive testing will be challenged in the UK.

Standard administration can also be achieved through the use of sound and/or video recordings produced to professional standards. Applicants can be given a general welcome after which the recording is started. As well as the general instructions and practice, for example, timing can be recorded too. Such an approach has potential when testing is carried out at a number of locations.

Scoring
Small business and other computers can score tests at high speed, and this is nearly always done if the test is administered on a computer. For tests that are administered in a pencil-and-paper forms, special answer sheets can be designed; subsequently, by means of a document reader, the replies on the answer sheets can be transferred into a computer. As well as scoring, there is often the facility to show how an individual score relates to a reference group – this is done by means of the percentile scores, the allocation of scores to grades, etc. Some computer bureaux and university and polytechnic departments can offer facilities for document reading and analysis on a consultancy basis.

The main potential disadvantage of computerised scoring concerns its reliability when, in particular, the equipment is used for the first time (see the earlier section on Test Development). In addition, the special equipment for 'reading' replies on printed answer sheets is sufficiently expensive for a high through-put of testing to be necessary for it to pay its way. Accordingly, it may only make financial sense to keep such equipment at a central point rather than have a number of machines at all the places where testing may be carried out.

Interpretation

Scoring can end with the production of a series of test scores for an individual. For an aptitude test this might include 'raw score' (usually the number of correct items), and the percentile score. For a personality questionnaire, the results might be given in the form of raw scores on a number of personality traits or other dimensions, and a profile might be produced so that the salient personality features for each individual can be seen with relative ease. In both instances the results may then be passed to a psychologist or personnel manager trained in testing who may make a decision on the basis of the results and his or her background knowledge about the tests; alternatively, and perhaps more likely, such assessors may seek to collect further relevant information during later stages of the assessment procedure (eg at interview) before making a decision.

However, the scoring need not end with a numerical summary being provided for human decision-making. In some ways it is a relatively small step to print additional words (such as pass and fail) alongside the aptitude test results, basing the printed judgement on a decision-making model supplied by the person running or organising the testing programme. In fact computers have been used to develop much more elaborate schemes; for example, one long-established personality questionnaire has become the basis of a computer print-out about susceptibility to stress, while other schemes are attempting to give information about jobs and careers that an individual may consider on the basis of aptitude tests and questionnaire replies.

Such schemes have their attractions since the computers can be programmed to take into account systematically large amounts of information both about people and about potential jobs. Thus large numbers of people can be systematically processed and skilled staff need not be involved.

On the other hand, there is much to be questioned. First, there are the normal questions to be asked about the level of confidence that can be placed in the test scores or questionnaire replies. Next there is the level of confidence that can be placed in the descriptions of the available jobs, particularly as individuals can differ in their views about the attractions and disadvantages of the same job. Third, there is the issue

159

of the decision-making model that is being used. Whose model is it? Has the model been agreed by a group of recognised experts, or does it represent the views of a single unqualified individual?

At best, computer-generated reports are produced by 'expert systems' which not only consider the score on each scale or dimension but also assess the total picture of personality that is being given in the way that a trained and experienced assessor may look for patterns which support each other, patterns which conflict, and so on. But even then some psychologists are of the view that personality questionnaire results are best used as a starting point for possible lines of enquiry and discussion during an interview rather than a firm and permanent picture of personality. Such psychologists would argue that even if a full print-out is available it is best restricted to experienced assessors able to interpret the questionnaire without the computer interpretation; in this way the print-out becomes a possible short cut to an assessment rather than a blind act of faith.

However, the vast majority of computer-generated reports or narratives are actually rather simple affairs in which the program simply prints out a couple of descriptive statements in relation to each trait according to whether the individual has scored high, medium or low on it. While these may be organised together under broader headings that they might relate to, the computer programs are unable to cope with, or comment on, combinations of scores – for example, they would not directly spell out the different behavioural implications of someone having a high score on impulsiveness and spontaneity as well as a high score on aggression compared to a low score on impulsiveness and a high degree of personal control as well as the high score on aggression. This kind of simple computer-based system – and it probably represents the majority – is thus quite crude and does not offer a very fine-grained analysis and interpretation, even though it may look quite sophisticated at first glance.

Monitoring

Among activities that need to be carried out, and that are speeded up by the use of small business or other computers, are the following:

- the establishment of text norms for the organisation or site (so that these can be compared with those for other organisations)
- the establishment of norms for subgroups of applicants (eg by age, sex, ethnic origin) to check that these tests are 'fair'

- the comparison of information about the test scores of individuals and the performance of the same individuals during training and subsequently on the job (see Chapter 9).

Government legislation

Most of this has been described earlier in the book (see Chapter 3), including the one major development since the last edition, namely the Disability Discrimination Act 1995. The other notable feature of recent times is that the legislation dealing with unfair discrimination on grounds of race or gender has been invoked more often in the testing field (Pickard, 1996), and this is likely to continue. There are, however, some other changes that may impact on testing practices in the near future. The influence of European Union legislation could well increase, and have ramifications that are as yet unclear. For example, the question of whether tests may act as a barrier to the free movement of labour within the EU has been raised; if it were judged that they did, this would fall foul of EU law. There is also the possibility of legislation on age discrimination at some future date; scores on many tests do vary with age to a limited extent – but so does job performance!

The role of The BPS in promoting higher standards of test use

The most ambitious steps to improving the way tests are used have been those taken by The British Psychological Society, partly at the instigation of the IPD, by introducing the assessment of competence in psychological testing. The first stage of this, the Level A statement of competence in occupational testing, dealt specifically with ability tests. The next stage, which was rather delayed and began to be implemented only in the mid-1990s, was the introduction of the Level B competence scheme. This deals with the use of personality and interest measures. It represents a requirement for substantial breadth and depth of knowledge of underlying theory and principles to be certified as competent in personality testing (indeed, Level A is a prerequisite before even starting Level B). Previously, it was sufficient to attend the relevant test suppliers' courses, which understandably tended to be more narrowly focused on the particular personality measure in question. While such courses are still obviously necessary, they do not in themselves provide an adequate basis for full Level B competence.

Ultimately, however, all this effort to raise standards depends for its success on the desire of test users to increase their competence and expertise. Those purveying tests of doubtful quality are only too quick to offer them without any questions asked; indeed, they would probably prefer to be selling to customers who have not attained the Level B competence, because anyone who has is more likely to identify unsound tests and to reject them anyway. The number of personnel staff who seek to achieve Level B competence will perhaps be a good yardstick by which to judge the extent to which there is a genuine desire within the profession to improve practice in the difficult area of personality assessment. At the time of writing, it is too early to say what the take-up will be.

The other, associated step, is the publication of Test Reviews by The BPS. These have been mentioned earlier in the book (see page 31).

Current issues and trends in psychological testing

In a discipline that is moving at the speed of this one, it can be a somewhat uncertain undertaking to try to identify trends and to speculate on developments. Here are some that are worth mentioning.

Trends in types of measures available and used
The vast majority of new psychometric instruments being produced are personality measures. These not only include updates and revisions of well-established questionnaires, but also completely new omnibus measures of personality (ie questionnaires yielding scores on a whole range of personality traits). This suggests that 'attacks' on the use of such measures have had absolutely no impact. While this continued growth is largely a reflection of demand, it is also stimulated in part by academic research showing some consensus on what are the main and most consistent features of personality that we should be concentrating on. These are the so-called 'big five' personality traits (extraversion, neuroticism, openness to experience, conscientiousness, and agreeableness) and their component elements. Of these, conscientiousness does seem particularly important in predicting success in work settings; it is also related to the assessment of integrity, described below.

Apart from these general personality measures, new assessment instruments do seem to focus on a few popular themes. One is sales ability or aptitude, and customer-orientation; many new measures in this area have appeared fairly recently. Some of these tests are very specific in application (eg SPQ Gold, which is focused on cold-call telesales) and some are much more general (eg the Poppleton-Allan Sales Aptitude Test, known as PASAT). Another significant development is a re-kindling of interest in motivation. Personality traits may describe some consistent features of an individual's behaviour, but they do not explain what lies behind it – what the key drivers are for this person. Although the concept of motivation is a distinctly tricky one for psychologists, it is certainly something that is meaningful in terms of everyday descriptions of behaviour, and it is clearly of interest to organisations. There have been few tests that have ventured into this area since the 1930s and 1940s, but some of the major test producers have introduced new motivation measures fairly recently.

Perhaps the most controversial addition to the psychometric armoury are integrity tests. The Michigan Employability Survey (1989) found that employers were becoming increasingly concerned about the integrity of their employees. Of the 86 employee qualities ranked for importance in entry-level employment, seven of the top eight qualities were related to integrity, trustworthiness and conscientiousness. The majority of research literature that cites the costs of employee theft, fraud and other counterproductive behaviour to organisations comes from the USA. However, it is increasingly clear that UK employers share the same concerns, though they tend to remain very secretive about the methods they are using to assess honesty. One indicator of this is that major test producers in the UK are turning their attention to the production of measures relevant to these concerns: the first British example is a questionnaire called Giotto, marketed by The Psychological Corporation.

The term 'integrity' as applied within the workplace covers many aspects of employee behaviour – from that which is against civil law (theft, fraud and embezzlement), against company law (absenteeism, malingering and tardiness) and against the norms of behaviour that are established within a work unit (not 'pulling your weight'). Integrity tests are usually differentiated into two general categories of *overt* or *covert* tests (Sackett and Harris, 1984), or into direct and indirect measures. The distinction between them arises from what the test producers, on the basis of research findings, see to offer strongest predictive power. On the one hand, there is substantial evidence that past behaviour is indicative of future behaviour, as are the attitudes we hold about acceptable behaviour (Cunningham *et al*, 1994). This is reflected in overt integrity test items, which question respondents on their perceptions of specific behaviours in hypothetical situations, as well as directly questioning whether they have committed certain acts of deviance in the past.

On the other hand, covert integrity tests assess certain personality traits of respondents; research has indicated that there is a very strong relationship between an individual's level of integrity and level of conscientiousness (Ash, 1991). Conscientious employees are hard-working, reliable, dependable and thorough (Murphy and Lee, 1994). As such, they are less likely to engage in counter-productive behaviour, and on the assumption that individuals are more likely to violate work unit norms before civil law, are also less likely to engage in more serious acts of deviance.

Test publishers of overt and covert integrity tests often claim that the tests can accurately predict very specific forms of dishonest behaviour – most commonly theft of cash or stock (Camara and Schneider, 1995). The debate over the extent to which the claims of test producers are met (ie the predictive validity of integrity tests) has raged for a number of years (see Ones *et al*, 1996 for further discussion). In light of the research evidence, the best advice would seem to urge that psychometric measures of integrity should be used with extreme caution – the decision to reject a candidate because they pose a high risk of engaging in deviant or dishonest behaviour is a conclusion that should be arrived at on the basis of more than just their score on one test (Baldry and Fletcher, 1997). Many researchers in this field have suggested the use of weighted application blanks (ie extra weighting being given to certain biographical details which have been found to correlate to an individual's level of integrity), so that very high-risk individuals can be screened out at the beginning of the recruitment process, thereby saving time and money for the organisation and reducing the level of disappointment felt by rejected applicants. Also, there are other, more traditional, assessment techniques that have the potential to contribute to assessing integrity – including references, interviews and simulation exercises (see Fletcher, 1995 for a discussion).

Perhaps most fundamentally, though, is the need keep in mind that integrity and honesty are not completely stable and consistent aspects of an individual's behaviour. Many situational influences, including management practices and ethos, will interact with individual predispositions to determine the degree of honesty shown. So, achieving high levels of integrity in an organisation is not only (perhaps not even primarily) a selection problem; integrity is likely to grow and develop in healthy organisations (Newell, 1995) that practise as well as promote it through their HR policies and their attitude to wider aspects of organisational citizenship.

Two further developments of the types of measures being used are worth mentioning. These are measures of team-working and of organisational culture. To some extent, these are of course related and reflect a desire to go beyond the individual and to direct psychometric measurement to wider issues in organisational effectiveness. Team role measures are of course not new, but many more are appearing now and often with a wider developmental focus. The measures of organisational climate and of organisational commitment are more for use in measuring employee attitudes as a barometer of reactions to change, diagnosing internal problems and so on. Research shows that they can accurately reflect differences between organisations in terms of the effectiveness of their HR systems (Fletcher and Williams, 1996; Audit Commission, 1995b).

Trends in how tests are used
One aspect of test use is the reliance placed on them. While there appear to be fewer new cognitive ability tests being produced, there is every indication that they are becoming more, and not less, influential in assessment decision-making. One might reasonably surmise that some recent changes and outputs from the educational system are responsible for the even greater reliance being put on these measures. Steadily improving GCSE and A level results, a greater number of students going to university and higher proportions of them gaining 'good' degrees, have led to uncertainty in some employers' minds about whether standards are genuinely higher or assessment standards lower. Either way, if a higher proportion of students get higher grades, then higher grades may become less effective as a way of differentiating between them – leading to a search for other, additional, ways of assessing intellectual capacity. Given all this, it is no surprise if some employers place more trust in cognitive ability test results.

The other general aspect of test use that has changed in recent years is the way they are now commonly related to assessment, couched in the terminology of company competency frameworks. This is not at all straightforward, though. The cause of the difficulty is that competency frameworks and psychological test dimensions usually describe behaviour at different levels. An individual competency description typically focuses on a broad pattern of surface behaviour relating to some aspect of work performance, eg organisation and planning. This will then be described in terms of positive and negative behaviours like 'can link own plans with wider strategic objectives', 'prioritises demands made on his time', 'carefully monitors progress', 'initiates action without thinking it through' (all these are taken from actual examples of descriptors for such a competency). When the psychologist looks at this range of behaviour, several different psychological constructs are likely to seem relevant – thoughtfulness, analytical thinking, caution, impulsiveness and so on. In other words, the psychological dimensions are often much narrower in nature, and several different ones may be relevant to any one competency. Even with very work-focused personality measures, such as the OPQ, this remains true.

So, it becomes quite complicated to line up the psychological test dimensions with the competencies. In a few cases, there are actually no very clear or close relationships between the two; competencies that revolve around the notion of business sense or business awareness often come into this category. More usually, though, a number of psychological constructs look to be relevant to each competency. This may raise a problem, in that it is common to find that no single psychometric test fits the bill – not one of them will offer measures of all the psychological dimensions that the analysis of the competency framework throws up. This being the case, the choice is either to use several different tests – not attractive in terms of time or cost – or to decide to prioritise and perhaps use just one or two tests that cover most of what you are interested in; the latter is normally the course adopted.

A second, tougher, issue can arise if the psychological analysis of what is involved in the competencies suggests that the competencies do not make psychological sense. Either the psychological qualities required for different behaviours described under a single competency conflict with each other, or the same thing is true across two (or more) different competencies – implying that it is unlikely that an individual could be high on both. By way of illustration, take a competency called achievement orientation; the behavioural descriptions frequently include such things as 'sets targets beyond those required', and 'wants to be the best'. The psychological profile for individuals with very strong achievement motivation is not always one that fits very comfortably with the teamwork and interpersonal competencies, which often emphasise the capacity to put personal credit to one side in favour of the team, or imply giving higher priority to team cohesion and individual well-being than to personal goals.

Finally, a third possible problem stems from almost the opposite phenomenon, namely the same psychological factors contributing to different competencies. A common example would be a trait like emotional control contributing to the assessment of competencies such as customer relations, resilience, interpersonal sensitivity, and so on. Having the same psychological factors relating to different competencies can cause problems in being able to discriminate between the latter and assess them independently.

166

It seems that tests do not translate into competencies all that easily. Sometimes, the problem lies in the quality of the original work done in identifying the competencies. But in other cases it goes deeper, and reflects an unrealistic expectation of what people can achieve. The underlying assumption of some frameworks is that the competencies are all compatible and that it is possible to be strong in all of them. Psychologically, there are grounds for challenging this assumption. More pragmatically, though, the advice might be to leave plenty of time to think through the use of tests in this context, and to realise that they seldom map neatly on to competencies – other assessment methods will be needed.

Trends in the developmental potential of tests

One of the least satisfactory aspects of test use has been the failure to exploit the developmental value of the results for the individual and the organisation. Perhaps part of the problem was the lack in many companies of in-house expertise to do this. It is encouraging to see that tests are increasingly accompanied by various devices that help in this direction. They may come with computer generated reports that focus specifically on the developmental implications of the data or, better still, have associated training techniques (ranging from tapes and workbooks all the way through to dedicated training courses) geared to the test profile of the candidate. This approach is particularly evident in the measures of sales aptitude that are now available, and could usefully be spread further.

Keeping informed about future developments

Within the UK, the main source of information about aptitude and other tests comes from psychologists whose professional organisation is The British Psychological Society (for address see page xiv). Leading occupational psychologists belong to the Division of Occupational Psychology, which vets people's experience and competence as practitioners before accepting them as members, and from 1988 its members became chartered occupational psychologists. Readers are strongly advised to employ only psychologists with this qualification, whose names and addresses appear in a register published by The BPS.

The British Psychological Society also publishes the *Selection and Development Review*, a journal devoted to the critical review of assessment methods, and other articles covering practical and political ussues relating to assessment and counselling. It also contains up-to-date information on courses in testing to be held during the following two to three months, and reviews of recent academic research of relevance.

The BPS also publishes an academic journal called *The Journal of Occupational and Organizational Psychology* and runs conferences and other events for psychologists; non-psychologists can attend many conferences and other events by invitation; some of these conferences and events cover the use of psychological tests and related methods such as assessment centres.

International organisations may find it helpful to keep in touch with psychological societies, test publishers and leading consultants in the countries in which they are operating. Such information is available from the International Test Commission, whose objectives are to compare practices in the use of tests throughout the world.

This book has been published under the auspices of the Institute of Personnel and Development which has some 88,000 members in the United Kingdom. Articles on the use of tests are published in its monthly publication, *People Management*, and the IPD also runs courses on the use of tests and on other selection procedures. Details of IPD courses in the use of psychological tests are available from the Institute's Course and Conference Department. Further details about leading test publishers are available in the form of an information note from the IPD's Information and Advisory Services Department. Because these details change from time to time, they are not reproduced in full in this book, but details of the suppliers of tests described in Chapter 2 are given in Appendix 4.

References

AMERICAN PSYCHOLOGICAL ASSOCIATION. (1985) *Standards of Educational and Psychological Testing*. Washington DC, APA.

ANASTASI, A. (1982) *Psychological Testing*. 5th edn. New York, Macmillan.

ASH, P. (1991) *The construct of employee theft proneness*. Park Ridge, IL, SRA/London House.

AUDIT COMMISSION. (1995b) *Management Handbook: Paying the piper and calling the tune*. London, HMSO.

BALDRY, C. and FLETCHER, C. (1997) 'The integrity of integrity testing'. *Selection and Development Review*. 13. pp3–6.

BARTRAM, D. (1995) *Review of Personality Assessment Instruments (Level B) for Use in Occupational Settings*. Leicester, BPS Books.

BEDFORD, T and FELTHAM, R. T. (1986) *A Cost Benefit Analysis of the Extended Interview Method*. Home Office Unit at CSSB Report No.2. London, The Home Office.

BELBIN, R. M. (1981) *Management Teams: Why they succeed or fail*. London, Heinemann.

BENTZ, V. J. (1985) 'Research findings from personality assessment of executives', in H. G. Bernadin and D. A. Bownas (eds), *Personality Assessment in Organisations*, New York, Praeger.

BOYATSIS, R. E. (1982) *The Competent Manager*. New York, John Wiley and Sons.

CAMARA, W. J. and SCHNEIDER, D. L. (1995) 'Questions of construct breadth and openness of research in integrity testing'. *American Psychologist*. 50. pp459–60.

CRONBACH, L. J. (1984) *Essentials of Psychological Testing*. 4th edn. New York, Harper and Row.

CUNNINGHAM, M. R., WONG, D. T. *and* BARBEE, A. P. (1994) 'Self-presentation dynamics on overt integrity tests: experimental studies of the Reid Report'. *Journal of Applied Psychology*. Vol.79, No.5. pp643–58.

DULEWICZ, S. V. (1989) 'Assessment centres as the route to competence'. *Personnel Management*. November. pp56–9.

DULEWICZ, S. V. (1991) 'Improving the effectiveness of assessment centres'. *Personnel Management*. June. pp50–55.

DULEWICZ, S. V. (1997) *Personal Competencies Framework: User's Manual*. Windsor, NFER-Nelson.

FLETCHER, C. (1985) 'Feedback of psychometric test results: how great is the demand?' *Guidance and Assessment Review*. No.6, December. pp1–2.

FLETCHER, C. (1986) 'Should the test score be kept a secret?' *Personnel Management*. April. pp44–6.

FLETCHER, C. (1995) 'What means to assess integrity?' *People Management*. August. pp30–31.

FLETCHER, C. *and* WILLIAMS, R. (1996) 'Performance management, job satisfaction and organisational commitment'. *British Journal of Management*. 7. pp169–79.

FRENCH, C. C. (1986) 'Microcomputers and psychometric assessment'. *British Journal of Guidance and Counselling*. Vol.14, No. 1. pp33–45.

GAUGLER, B., ROSENTHAL, D., THORNTON G. *and* BENTSON C. (1987) 'Meta analysis of assessment centre validity'. *Journal of Applied Psychology*. Vol.72, No.3. pp493–511.

GHISELLI, E. E. (1966) *The Validity of Occupational Aptitude Tests*. New York, John Wiley and Sons.

HUNTER, J. E. *and* SCHMIDT, F. L. (1982) 'The economic benefits of personnel selection using psychological ability tests'. *Industrial Relations*.

170

ILES, P. A. *and* ROBERTSON, I. T. (1995) 'The impact of personnel selection procedures on candidates', in N. ANDERSON and P. HERRIOT (eds), *Assessment and Selection in Organisations: Second update*. London, John Wiley and Sons.

INSTITUTE OF PERSONNEL AND DEVELOPMENT. (1997) *The IPD Guide on Psychological Testing*. London, IPD.

JOHNSON, C., SAVILLE, P. *and* FLETCHER, C. (1989) 'A test by any other name'. *Personnel Management*. March. pp47–51.

JONES, R. (1990) 'Integrating selection in a merged company'. *Personnel Management*. September. pp38–42.

KLIMOSKI, R. J. *and* RAFAELI, A. (1983) 'Inferring personal qualities through handwriting analysis'. *Journal of Occupational Psychology*. Vol.56. pp191–202.

KLINE, P. (1986) *A Handbook of Test Construction*. London, Methuen.

LEWIS, C. (1985) *Employee Selection*. London, Hutchinson.

LOUNSBURY, J. W., BOBROW, W. *and* JENSEN, J. B. (1989) 'Attitudes to employment testing: scale development, correlates and "known group" validation'. *Professional Psychology: Research and practice*. 20. Pp340–49.

MCCORMICK, E. J. *and* ILGEN, D. (1985) *Industrial Psychology*. 8th edn. London, Allen and Unwin.

Michigan Employability Survey (1989) in *The Use of Integrity Tests for Pre-Employment Screening* (1990), The Office of Technology Assessment, US Congress, Washington DC.

MILLER, K. M. (ed.) (1975) *Psychological Testing in Personnel Assessment*. Aldershot, Gower Press.

MOSES, J. L. (1985) 'Using clinical methods in a high level management assessment centre', in Bernadin, H. G. and Bownas, D. S. (eds), *Personality Assessment in Organisations*, New York, Praeger.

MURPHY, K. R. *and* LEE, S. L. (1994) 'Personality variables related to integrity test scores: the role of conscientiousness'. *Journal of Business and Psychology*. Vol.8, No.4. pp413–24.

NEWELL, S. (1995) *The Healthy Organization*. London, Routledge.

ONES, D. S., SCHMIDT, F. L., VISWESVARAN, C. *and* LYKKEN, D. T. (1996) 'Controversies over integrity testing: two viewpoints'. *Journal of Business and Psychology*. Vol.10, No.4. pp487–501.

PEARN, M. (1979) *The Fair Use Of Tests*. Windsor, NFER-Nelson.

PICKARD, J. (1996) 'The wrong turns to avoid with tests'. *People Management*. 9 August. pp20–25.

ROBERTSON, I. T. *and* MAKIN, P. J. (1986) 'Management selection in Britain: a survey and critique'. *Journal of Occupational Psychology*. Vol.59, No.1. pp45–58.

RODGER, A. (1953) *The Seven Point Plan*. Windsor, NFER-Nelson.

RYNES, S. L. (1993) 'Who's selecting whom? Effects of selection practices on applicant attitudes and behavior', in N. Schmitt, W. Borman and Associates (eds), *Personnel Selection in Organizations*, San Francisco CA, Jossey-Bass.

RYNES, S. L. *and* CONNERLY M. L., (1993) 'Applicant reactions to alternative selection procedures'. *Journal of Business and Psychology*. 7. pp261–77.

RYNES, S. L., HENEMAN, H. G. *and* SCHWAB, D. P. (1980) 'Individual reactions to organisational recruiting: a review'. *Personnel Psychology*. Vol.33. pp529–42.

SACKETT, P. R. *and* HARRIS, M. M. (1984) 'Honesty testing for personnel selection: a review and critique'. *Personnel Psychology*. 37. pp221–45.

SCHMIDT, F. L. *and* HUNTER, J. E. (1979) 'The impact of valid selection procedures on workforce productivity'. *Journal of Applied Psychology*. 64. pp609–26.

SHACKLETON, V. J. *and* FLETCHER, C. (1984) *Individual Differences: Theories and applications*. London, Methuen.

SHACKLETON, V. J. *and* NEWELL, S. (1991) 'Management Selection: A comparative survey of methods used in top British and French companies'. *Journal of Occupational Psychology*. Vol.64. pp23–36.

SILVESTER, J. *and* BROWN, A. (1993) 'Graduate recruitment: testing the impact'. *Selection and Development Review*. Vol.9, No.1. pp1–3.

SMITH, M. (1986) 'Selection: where are the best prophets?' *Personnel Management*. p63.

SOCIETY FOR INDUSTRIAL AND ORGANIZATIONAL PSYCHOLOGY. (1987). *Principles for the Validation and Use of Personnel Selection Procedures*. Maryland MD, the University of Maryland.

STAGNER, R. (1958) 'The gullibility of personnel managers'. *Personnel Psychology*. Vol.11. pp347–52.

THORNTON, C. G. *and* BYHAM, W. C. (1982) *Assessment Centres and Managerial Performance*. New York, Academic Press.

TOPLIS, J. W. (1970) 'Studying people at work'. *Journal of Occupational Psychology*. 44. pp95–114.

TOPLIS, J. W. *and* STEWART, B. (1983) 'Group selection methods', in B. Ungerson (ed.), *Recruitment Handbook*, 3rd edn, Aldershot, Gower Press.

TYLER, B. *and* MILLER, K. (1986) 'The use of tests by psychologists: report on a survey of BPS members'. *Bulletin of the British Psychological Society*. Vol 39. pp405–10.

WOLFF, C. J., de (1989). 'The changing role of psychologists in selection', in P. Herriot (ed.), *Assessment and Selection in Organisations*, Chichester, John Wiley and Sons.

WOODRUFFE, C. (1990) *Assessment Centres*. London, Institute of Personnel and Development.

Appendix 1
Choosing psychological tests:
A case-study

Chapter 6 describes a number of issues to be taken into account when choosing a test. In the real world, of course, sufficient information seldom exists about an off-the-shelf test to recommend its immediate and unqualified use. On the other hand, few employing organisations are likely to be prepared to spend months if not years waiting for the results of predictive evaluation exercises before deciding what test or tests to use.

Recent projects carried out by Post Office psychologists have sometimes involved a concurrent validation study as a method of deciding which tests to use. The following case-study illustrates this approach in practice. Details are summarised from 'The value of test validation: a case study', a paper prepared for publication by Dr David Kellett, Ira Morris and Deirdre Fitzgerald.

The aim of the project was to recommend tests for the selection of clerical-grade staff, if possible from among the batteries available off-the-shelf from commercial publishers because of the time and cost involved in designing a new test from scratch. The project began with job analyses of all the clerical duties in the main functional areas such as personnel, customer services, finance, operations, buildings and services. Psychologists carried out interviews lasting up to one and a half hours as well as working through the job components inventory, and a list of 29 activities was drawn up.

Commercially available tests were then reviewed in the light of the job requirements, and two test batteries – the Clerical Abilities Battery from The Psychological Corporation and the Modern Occupational Skills tests from Assessment for Selection and Employment (ASE) – appeared the most promising. These two batteries were then evaluated in detail against a number of quality standards (see Kellett and Toplis, 1989). Considering the contents of the test batteries, and evidence about their reliability, validity and fairness, it was concluded that the Modern Occupational Skills Battery was the better suited on this occasion.

However, the Modern Occupational Skills battery comprises nine separate tests, all with high 'face validity'. The next question to be considered was how many needed to be used. An analysis revealed that all nine tests were significantly correlated with each other, the highest being a correlation of 0.72. This was a clear sign that not all the tests would be necessary since, if two tests correlate highly, there is unlikely to be value in using both.

The next step was to compare scores on all the tests with supervisors' ratings of each individual's performance on the 29 clerical activities that had been identified. A technique called step-wise regression analysis was used to see whether any other tests in the battery added significantly to the ability of the best test to predict supervisors' ratings of performance.

Results showed that a small number of tests appeared to be useful predictors of many of the supervisors' ratings – for example, two of the tests were each useful predictors of 11 supervisor ratings. In contrast, some tests in the battery were of relatively little value. It seemed likely that the best value for money would be obtained by using just three of the nine tests.

A final step before the tests were released for operational use was to look at the fairness of the tests. Insufficient numbers from the ethnic minorities volunteered to take part in the concurrent validation study, so the checking of race fairness has had to be postponed until the predictive validation study.

So far as the sex fairness of the tests was concerned, data were examined to see whether there were (a) sex differences in the means scores and (b) whether there were differences in the correlation between test score and performance according to the sex of those tested. Findings for the three tests that had shown most promise were as follows:

	Comparison of mean scores (m/f)	*Comparison of correlations (m/f)*
Test 1	no difference	no difference
Test 2	no difference	no difference
Test 3	m slightly higher	m slightly higher

At the same time, data for all the other tests in the MOST battery were analysed in a similar way. Some differences were found with two other tests which would mean that they would require careful monitoring had they been included in the final battery. These findings have been passed on to the test publishers.

In the light of the above findings it was decided to press ahead with the introduction of the tests. However, their use is being carefully monitored, and a predictive validation study and further work on race and sex fairness will be carried out as soon as sufficient data have accumulated.

The study shows the value of careful preliminary work before tests are introduced. The nine tests in the MOST battery all have high 'face validity' and, without the study, it would have been impossible to say which tests were the more effective, how many were required in the final battery, and whether or not they required careful monitoring for race or sex fairness.

John Toplis

Reference

KELLETT, D. *and* TOPLIS, J. (1989) 'Quality standards for the development and use of psychological tests'. *Guidance and Assessment Review*, Vol. 5, No. 4. pp4–8.

Appendix 2
Retaining or employing occupational psychologists

Personnel managers and others who expect large-scale benefits from the introduction of testing would be well advised to seek expert advice on the choice, introduction, use, interpretation and evaluation of psychological tests.

At present, the best single guide as to whether or not an individual is expert in psychological testing for selection and assessment at work is whether he or she is included in Index 3 of the *Directory of Chartered Occupational Psychologists*, which is published annually by the Occupational Division of The British Psychological Society; Index 3 contains those chartered occupational psychologists specialising in personnel selection and assessment, and covers analysing selection requirements, skills in application form design, interviewing, and assessment techniques such as the design and use of psychometric tests and exercises, and expertise in the design and running of assessment centres. For particular assignments, inclusion in some of the other indexes in the *Directory* may be relevant too – for example, Index 4 (Performance Appraisal and Career Development) or Index 5 (Counselling and Personal Development).

Dealing with chartered occupational psychologists who are members of the Division of Occupational Psychology has two further advantages. First, election to membership takes account of the breadth of experience of members, and this can be important if improvements in selection methods are only one of the possible ways of resolving an organisation's problems. Faced with problems such as low output or high labour turnover, it is often important to identify the most cost-effective solutions; improving selection methods may or may not be the best way forward (Toplis, 1970). A second advantage is that those appearing in the *Directory* have agreed to follow the code of conduct for chartered psychologists and the code of professional conduct of the Division of Occupational Psychology, both designed to benefit those seeking advice.

A few psychologists with considerable experience in occupational testing and assessment do not appear in the *Directory*, but there are a number of other ways of checking their credibility; some of the following points may also be helpful for assessing any chartered occupational psychologists who may have been shortlisted. For example, is the individual:

- a chartered psychologist with a background in a different specialism of psychology? (A register of all chartered psychologists is available from The British Psychological Society)

- registered with an overseas psychological society at a level of membership equivalent to chartered psychologist?

- an associate member of The British Psychological Society (a grade to which ordinary – graduate – members of the Society can be elected)?

- involved in any of the committees of The British Psychological Society?

- involved in the publication of papers in refereed scientific journals such as the *Journal of Occupational Psychology*?

A period of employment with a major employer of occupational psychologists (such as the Civil Service Commission, the Post Office, British Telecom or British Airways) might also be a good sign, as would a period of employment in a recognised academic institution. However, always check that the individual has been employed as a psychologist and that he or she has been supervised by a chartered psychologist.

For organisations with large-scale programmes of staff recruitment and assessment there can be considerable advantages in employing one or more chartered occupational psychologists, not only for the advice they can give *vis-à-vis* the organisation's problems, but also the advice they can give on the many selection and assessment methods that organisations are pressed to trial and use (see Chapter 1). For the most part, those who design and sell unproven techniques claim little association with professional psychology in the UK, and may even claim this as a merit!

Finally, remember that some people offering advice on the use of tests may be holders of the certificate of competence in occupational testing (Level A) whose training will fall far short of the three to five years postgraduate experience required of those wishing to become chartered occupational psychologists. Verification of their claim to the certificate can be made by reference to the register held by The British

Psychological Society or by a telephone call to the Society. While such people may have considerable experience of the use of a few tests, they will not normally have the range of background information about tests or the statistical skills to give comprehensive advice, nor are they likely to have access to a wide range of Level B tests, including personality questionnaires.

John Toplis

Appendix 3
A brief overview of the theory of mental abilities

When psychological tests are mentioned, the public still tends to think about intelligence or IQ tests, even though the trend for the last two or three decades has been moving away from an overall intelligence measure towards measures of more specific abilities. Although the early intelligence tests produced one overall score, many of them had subscales of similar items and psychologists started looking at variations of performance across these sub-scales, even though they were not sufficiently reliable to permit worthwhile interpretation.

The evidence for the existence of a general intelligence factor came from the work of Spearman, an English psychologist, in the early 1900s. He administered a wide range of different mental ability tests to a large group of people and, after statistical analysis (correlations) of the results, found a general ability spreading across the tests. People who got higher scores on one test tended also to do well on the others, and vice versa. The later development of a statistical technique called factor analysis, which permitted a more rigorous analysis of the results from various tests, enabled psychologists to identify much more specifically the independent factors (abilities) that are measured by a number of different tests (called a battery of tests). Unfortunately, however, different methods of factor analysis were developed and employed on either side of the Atlantic, resulting in different results and theories of mental ability, although these differences were not completely irreconcilable.

British psychologists, notably Burt and Vernon, proposed a hierarchical structure of human abilities, with the 'g', or general intelligence factor, accounting for most variation in performance across different tests. Once the effects of 'g' have been accounted for, it is possible to find two broad (major) groups of abilities:

- v:ed – standing for verbal and educational, and covering minor group factors such as verbal, numerical, memory and reasoning abilities

- k:m – standing for spatial (after El Kousi, an Egyptian psychologist) and mechanical abilities, as well as perceptual (sensory) and motor skills relating to physical operations such as eye–hand co-ordination and manual dexterity.

Once the effect of these three higher level factors have been accounted for, one is left with factors that are very test-specific. 'g' scores are very important for assessing someone's abilities to perform a broad range of jobs, or jobs requiring high intelligence (and also capacity to benefit from special education, eg the 11+ exam) whilst scores on minor group factors became more important for assessing people for specific jobs.

The US psychologists, on the other hand, to some extent as a result of their experience of using the early intelligence tests, used factor analytic methods in their research, which tended to emphasise differences between mental ability factors. In 1938 Thurstone identified seven ability factors which were relatively independent, although there were modest correlations between them. He named these factors primary mental abilities:

S   —   Spatial ability

P   —   Perceptual speed

N   —   Numerical ability

V   —   Verbal meaning

M   —   Memory

V   —   Verbal fluency

I/R   —   Inductive reasoning

Although much research has been carried out on these primary abilities in the intervening years the results have necessitated only minor modifications to the list of primary abilities. However, results from studies using certain factor analytic methods have shown that a general factor (intelligence) does emerge which is similar to the 'g' factor. The theoretical differences across the Atlantic are therefore not so great that they have undermined the efforts of practitioners in the assessment field.

Until the 1960s US test constructors were influenced mainly by Thurstone; their British counterparts by the work of Burt and Vernon. However, the model of human abilities devised by the US psychologist, Guilford, in the 1960s has probably had a significant influence on contemporary test constructors on both sides of the Atlantic. This model has three dimensions:

1 Mental operations:
    cognition
    memory
    divergent production (thinking)
    convergent production (thinking)
    evaluation.

2 Products:
    units
    classes
    relations
    systems
    transfunctions
    implications.

3 Contents:
    figural
    symbolic
    semantic
    behavioural.

In the model, tests have been sought to measure each cell across the three dimensions, eg a memory test dealing with classes of objects of a semantic (ie verbal) nature and so on.

At the time of his death, Guilford had claimed to have identified 98 factors out of the total possible 120 permutations across the three dimensions. His main influence on contemporary British test constructors has been on the development of tests involving different operations, relating to various ability levels of applicants; on the important differences between convergent (problem-solving) and divergent (lateral, creative) thinking; and clarification of 'products' and 'contents' measured by different tests.

Vic Dulewicz

Appendix 4
Suppliers of tests described in Chapter 2

1   The Morrisby Organisation
    83 High Street
    Hemel Hempstead
    Hertfordshire
    HP1 3AH
    01442-68645

2   ASE
    A division of NFER-Nelson
    Darville House
    2 Oxford Road East
    Windsor
    Berks
    SL4 1DF
    01753-850333

3   SHL
    Saville and Holdsworth Ltd
    3 AC Court
    High Street
    Thames Ditton
    Surrey
    KT7 0SR
    0181-398-4170

4   Oxford Psychologists Press Ltd
    Lambourne House
    311-321 Banbury Road
    Oxford
    OX2 7JH
    01865-510203

5   The Psychological Corporation Ltd
    24-28 Oval Road
    London
    NW1 7DX

6   The Test Agency
    Cray House
    Woodlands Road
    Henley-on-Thames
    Oxon
    RG9 4AE

There are a number of other test suppliers in the UK. The Institute of Personnel and Development keeps an up-to-date list of suppliers and copies can be sent to members on request.

Vic Dulewicz

Appendix 5
A review of The British Psychological Society Level A open learning programme

This programme aims to provide, via distance-learning materials, an alternative, more flexible, and cheaper way of acquiring Level A training than attending a course. It is also a very useful resource and reference work.

To obtain a certificate of competence at Level A it is necessary to convince an assessor that you have mastered the relevant material (as explained in Chapter 4), but it does not matter how that mastery has been achieved. For instance, it could be via private study, the open learning programme, a course or combination of courses, or a mixture of all of these. In practice most people are likely to go on a course specifically aimed at acquiring a Level A certificate, as this is the quickest and easiest route, if not the cheapest. In this case the assessment takes place on and/or at the end of the course.

If you have not attended a course but nevertheless feel that you are competent, perhaps because of following the open learning programme described here, you can find an assessor by contacting The British Psychological Society (address on page xiv). All assessors are chartered psychologists who are competent at Level A (and usually at the higher level too). Their standards are checked by a team of verifiers appointed by the BPS.

The open learning programme, which covers the whole of the Level A syllabus thoroughly, is undoubtedly a very useful resource and reference work, whether or not it is used as a major or the sole source of training.

The programme comprises seven distance-learning modules, three of them in two parts; an introduction and study guide, including a section on basic mathematical procedures and a glossary of terms; a test pack for practical work, including copies of a specially made test for practical use, administration instructions, conversion tables, candidate evaluation forms, etc; and an assessment portfolio intended as a record of performance on the various tasks set. The latter is particularly useful: it reproduces all the questions and exercises from the modules, with spaces for answers and notes, in one separate book. In addition to the material provided, it is necessary to have copies of the major test publishers' catalogues (see addresses in Appendix 4), and of the BPS Review of Psychometric Tests for Assessment in Vocational Training (Bartram *et al.*, 1990, with later updates).

The seven modules are: 1. Psychological Testing: an Introduction; 2. Scaling, Norms and Standardisation (2 parts); 3. Reliability and the Standard Error of Measurement (2 parts); 4. Validity and Fairness in Testing (2 parts); 5. Test Administration and Scoring; 6. Test Interpretation; 7. Choosing Tests. The modules cover The BPS Level A competences (decided on by a BPS Working Party), but do not exactly match these: for practical reasons the issues are handled in a different order.

The materials are well presented and relatively easy to find one's way around. The coverage is wide, and many complex and difficult-to-explain issues are put across clearly and thoroughly. There are a large, but not excessive, number of questions and exercises as one works through the texts. These are generally well chosen, involving real thought and not just regurgitation of the text. There are some excellent 'thinking questions' and practical exercises on, for example, norms. Clear and detailed answers are provided, but it is essential not to refer to these until the question has been thoroughly attempted.

The frequent graphical and diagrammatic representations will help many people, although a few could be puzzling, or even confusing, to certain (non-diagram-minded) students, who might understand more easily from the written text alone. However, in many cases diagrams of some sort are essential. There are also some good illustrative tables, including an interesting and useful example, explained in the text, of the problem of interpreting ipsative (forced choice questions) scores; this would be valuable to anyone wondering how to use forced choice scales since these are often interpreted incorrectly.

Being based on the BPS Level A competences, the programme naturally tends to reflect their strengths and weaknesses. It is very strong on all the technical issues, and also on what might be called theoretical and definitional matters. It is an excellent reference text for someone, even a chartered psychologist, who has completed Level A training.

The main weakness is in regard to certain practicalities. Some practical issues are covered very well, eg test administration, confidentiality, advance information to candidates, whilst others are relatively neglected, or the advice is presented in such a way that many people may feel that it represents an unattainable ideal. Whilst it is appropriate for such a programme to describe 'best practice', something to aim for (and not fall short of in matters such as standard instructions, good testing conditions, accurate scoring, etc), many readers may regard certain aspects as impractical, such as always giving full feedback to everyone tested, or always knowing if any ethnic differences have been found with a test. (In practice, if you ask publishers about such differences – as you should if there is little or nothing in the manual – you will find that some do not have – or perhaps will not disclose – this information.)

More importantly, the programme could put more emphasis on the difficult matter of actually choosing which test to use. Of course, in a sense, almost the whole text is concerned with this, but the most relevant points could have been brought together in one place in a more user-friendly way for managers and personnel practitioners. Perhaps understandably, there is also a tendency not to deal with cases where tests may not be appropriate.

The programme's strengths cause certain difficulties; the strong technical coverage means that some parts of the text may be quite daunting for non-mathematical readers. While the maths itself is not necessarily complex, some of the concepts and ideas will be completely new to most people, and the novel context may make the maths seem harder than it is. Moreover, the programme does go further than it strictly needs to (to cover the Level A units of competence); for example, it is probably unnecessary to have such theoretical and detailed coverage of the relationship between reliability and validity.

Occasionally, but not often enough, the text makes use of 'optional boxes' where a complex subject is explained further in an optional section. Other topics would also have benefited from this approach, for instance validity generalisation (the extent to which one can generalise from one or more validity studies to other contexts).

Students are asked to calculate certain statistics, such as correlations, as part of the learning process. Whilst this can certainly be a very good way to learn to use statistics (for conducting one's own validity studies for instance), performing calculations can also deter some people, and distract others from the more important matter, in this context, of understanding how to interpret them. In certain sections there is a great deal of computation, not all of it essential. While it is appropriate to warn readers about this, be assured that only occasionally is the material highly numerical.

The authors themselves warn that students are likely to need to spend considerable time on the difficult Modules 2 and 3 which, consisting of two parts each, and covering the technical background to test usage, do, in fact, constitute a major part of the programme in terms of length (and probably more in terms of time).

Once again reflecting the competences, the programme is also decidedly weak on the cost benefits of using tests, devoting only half a page or so to this directly. Issues of test acceptability, administrative practicality, etc are briefly dealt with, but financial aspects are hardly mentioned. The discussion of fairness in testing is very useful, particularly in the light of the fact that there are important legal issues to consider (avoiding unfair discrimination). It is unfortunate, although understandable, that it draws heavily on the USA where there has been much litigation and consideration of these matters; however it is UK and EU law that applies in the UK.

Despite these criticisms, this pack is an impressive and extremely useful set of learning materials. It is heartening to see some important and commonly misunderstood points made very clearly (eg validity is relative, not absolute; no instrument is valid in a vacuum – only in particular contexts); even those who have been on courses do not always understand these issues properly. However, many people are likely to have some difficulty with certain concepts in the programme, and with some of the numerical and graphical material. Because of this, it seems likely that the pack will most often be used in conjunction with other methods of learning. Short courses covering the more difficult issues may arise in response to demand, since a combination of distance and open learning and course attendance may well be a more effective way of assimilating material that is sometimes quite complex, than single, intensive, full-time courses.

Despite this, the latter will probably remain the commonest form of Level A training because of its convenience. For people trained in this way, particularly if they use tests only occasionally, these open learning materials would be very useful as a reference resource, to remind them of key points or of anything they have forgotten. The overviews, aims and summaries provided in each module are particularly helpful in this respect. In this context it is also worth reminding readers that this is a package of material covering the Level A competences published by The British Psychological Society, who are the custodians of testing standards in the UK (supported by the Institute of Personnel and Development), and written by two chartered psychologists who are not only well-regarded in this field, but who were directly involved with the production of the Level A (and Level B) competences, and with the creation of the BPS system of assessment and verification of standards.

Summary of The British Psychological Society Level A units of competence

NB. **The seven modules in the Level A pack do not follow exactly the seven units outlined here, ie the issues are covered in a different order etc. This is for practical reasons of effective teaching and dealing with issues in a logical order for students.**

Unit 1   Psychological testing: defining assessment needs

This unit deals with the general categorisation of types of assessment instrument and covers some underlying psychological theory and background to ability testing, eg general and specific abilities, influence of environmental factors. Job and task analysis are covered in so far as they relate to assessment; competence in job analysis is not assumed but ability to evaluate critically the results of job analyses is.

Unit 2   Basic principles of scaling and standardisation

This deals with the fundamental statistical concepts required to use psychological tests; most undergraduate psychology courses in the UK cover this material, as do some other social science courses, eg means, standard deviations, frequency distributions, sample size and standard error of the mean, confidence limits, percentiles, raw and standardised scores (Z-scores, T-scores, stens, stanines), using norms and conversion tables, ipsative and non-ipsative scales.

Unit 3   The importance of reliability and validity

This unit gives thorough coverage of the issues, including interpreting correlations obtained under different conditions, the basic premises of classical test theory ('true scores' and random error), pros and cons of different methods of estimating reliability, sources of error, effect of test length, range restriction and adjustments, standard error of measurement and how to use it, standard errors of difference between, and sum of, two scale scores, basic generalisability theory, types of validity and the relationship between reliability and validity, the extent to which one can generalise, pros and cons of different methods of assessing concurrent and predictive validity and the effects of selection on the latter.

Unit 4   Deciding when psychological tests should or should not be used as part of an assessment process

This unit covers a range of issues, some of which are expanded on in other units, eg the law relating to sex and ethnic discrimination; identifying suitable tests from catalogues and then, from the manuals, appropriate information regarding matters such as rationale, reliability, validity, norms, administration requirements and any restrictions on use; judging which test (if any) is most suitable and which norms; deciding how best to use the test(s) to maximise usefulness and minimise risks.

Unit 5   Administering tests to one or more candidates and dealing with scoring procedures

This is a very practical skill-based unit emphasising good professional practices in test administration, ensuring standard conditions and fairness. It includes practical planning and preparation, appropriate locations and advance information to candidates, security and confidentiality, different scoring methods, record sheets and norm tables.

Unit 6   Making appropriate use of test results and providing accurate written and oral feedback to clients and candidates

This unit stresses the interpersonal skills needed for face-to-face feedback as well as the oral and written communication skills required to convey technical information in lay terms, but accurately. It includes use of appropriate norms and cut-offs, suitably cautious interpretations, standard errors, placing norm-based scores in appropriate contexts, describing scores clearly, reflecting confidence limits (including the effect of correlation between scale scores), relating test performance to person-specification appropriately, computing composite test battery scores from weights provided, using appropriate and accurate language in describing tests and scales in lay terms, encouraging candidate participation in feedback sessions and their comments on the test(s) etc, issues of to whom and how information is presented, and clear guidance on the appropriate weight to attach to findings.

Unit 7   Maintaining security and confidentiality of the test materials and the test data

This covers the usual issues, including the Data Protection Act. Stress is

190

laid on making rights and obligations clear to clients and candidates, eg information on how results will be used, who will have access to them and for how long they will be retained.

Appendix 6
Assessing the worth of large correlations

In the early days of psychological testing, researchers and others tended to design tests to measure particular attributes and then went on to assess the worth of the test by correlating test scores against a performance criterion (eg scores on a test of mechanical aptitude against success as an apprentice). The correlations were carried out by hand and were slow and laborious to do.

Following on from this earlier work, there is still a widespread view among test users that correlations provide a way of deciding whether or not to use tests in a particular situation. However, times have changed in four ways:

- Many tests and questionnaires now produce *a series of scores* about each individual – one well-known personality questionnaire produces 30!

- It is now more common to collect *a number of measures* covering different aspects of job performance: quantity and quality of output, performance on different kinds of task, and so on.

- Many studies relating test scores to performance at work and other behaviour are no longer designed to test specific predictions; instead, researchers conduct 'fishing trips' through a mass of data to see if any interesting correlations can be found.

- The advent and widespread use of powerful small computers and statistical packages means that a mass of correlations can be carried out almost at the touch of a button.

Within the mass of correlations now being produced it is likely that some large and significant correlations will have occurred by change. The widespread view that correlations can help to identify tests which may be of value needs to change to meet these new circumstances.

In our view, test users and others making decisions about tests should look for evidence of worth over and above the *size* of correlation. Four kinds of evidence which could be considered are as follows:

- Is there evidence that the correlation has come from a scientifically rigorous study which has aimed to test *specific* predictions (hypotheses) about the relationship between test scores and performance? Such an approach is of particular importance when assessing the values of scales on personality questionnaires, each of which can be regarded as a separate test from the point of view both of making predictions and of subsequent statistical analysis.

- Is there evidence that an appropriate level of statistical significance has been applied to check that the correlation has not occurred by chance? For example, if a specific prediction or hypothesis is being tested, it might be appropriate to set a 5 per cent level of significance (ie that results would occur by chance only 5 times in 100); however, if 'evidence' comes from a large matrix of correlations (say, more than 50) and no specific predictions have been made in advance, a 2 per cent or even 1 per cent level of significance would seem more appropriate.

- Can researchers or others offer some theoretical or practical explanations for any large correlations that have been found?

- Have similar findings been made in independent studies – or can such independent studies be arranged? Unfortunately, finding evidence in the scientific literature is easier said than done, since journals and other publications have little interest in validation studies, let alone those studies that are not 'positive' in the sense of breaking new ground.

In the future, a fifth kind of evidence may be available. Sixty years ago, Wallace and Snedecor at Iowa State College published tables which showed the possibility of large correlations occurring by chance within correlation matrices, and Blinkhorn and Johnson are currently working along similar lines. This approach is valuable in alerting researchers and others to the possibility that correlations may be spurious, and may even help to identify those which are 'real'. However, proof based on theory, prediction, appropriate levels of statistical significance and replication is what is really required.

For further discussion of this issue, see the forum of expert views published by Clive Fletcher, Steve Blinkhorn *et al* as 'Personality tests: the great debate', *Personnel Management*, September 1991.

John Toplis
Victor Dulewicz
Clive Fletcher

Appendix 7
Meta-analysis and validity generalisation

For many years, psychologists and others were concerned about the apparent inconsistency in the worth of tests; a test could be a useful predictor in one situation, only to be found less effective, or even ineffective, in another. At one stage there was 'widespread acceptance of the "fact" that test validity was highly situation-specific, thus necessitating separate criterion-related validity studies for most situations' (Taylor, 1978).

This was not helpful either to psychologists or their clients and, during the last two decades, two possible ways forward have begun to be explored. First, Schmidt and Hunter suggested that situational specificity could be explained largely in terms of the small sample sizes employed in most previous validity research. They went on to suggest the use of a statistical procedure originating from educational research called meta-analysis to put together the findings from a number of studies and so get a better estimate of the true worth of a test.

A second approach concerned validity generalisation – finding ways of assessing the likely validity of a test in a new situation. There were basically two approaches to validity generalisation. The first approach is illustrated by Taylor and Colbert (1979), who became interested in whether it was possible to generalise about validity within particular job families. In their study, the Position Analysis Questionnaire was used to record details about a number of jobs in an insurance company. Factor analysis and other statistical techniques were then used to identify job families. Of the 13 families identified, they found that three of them contained jobs for which a substantial number of entry-level clerical personnel were hired, so they focussed their research on these three groups. They went on to find that test validity could be generalised within these three families.

Schmidt and Hunter (1977) originated the second approach to validity generalisation, which was based on the calculation of a figure for validity generalisability (transportability) dependent on two variables – the estimated mean true validity and the estimated standard deviation of true validities. The results of the calculation could determine whether or not validity was generalisable. However, the theoretical assumptions and methods of calculation were all debated at length in the scientific literature over the next decade.

The two basic concepts of meta-analysis and validity generalisation are still relevant today, although the underlying statistics have become very sophisticated and well beyond the scope of this book. One way of deciding whether to start to use, or continue to use, a particular test or other selection method is to consider the way that it has previously performed in similar situations. This way of making decisions can be useful if, for example:

- a decision has to be made between a number of tests designed for apparently similar work (eg clerical work)
- the number of people employed is so small that it does not make any sense to carry out a statistical study of the value of the test within your organisation alone.

There will be several sources of information about possible tests, including information from:

- the test publishers/distributors
- journals and other scientific publications
- occupational psychologists
- colleagues in the Institute of Personnel and Development.

For some tests quite detailed information may be available, including data from a number of independent studies about the correlations between test scores and subsequent performance. Until the early 1980s these might have been collected by test publishers and others as a series of narrative reviews. However, some findings may have been subjected to meta-analysis and an overall correlation for the studies as a whole computed.

In advocating meta-analysis as a way of more fairly judging the worth of tests, Schmidt and Hunter suggested that *at least 1,500* people should be involved in a study of the worth of a test if sampling and other errors were to be avoided. Such samples are very rarely found in practice. However, meta-analysis uses cumulative research to escape the problems of sampling error. If the average sample size in individual studies were 68 (as in personnel selection research), the 25 studies would produce a cumulative sample size of 1700 and, given other conditions, it should be possible to draw correct conclusions. A number of other statistical and research advantages were claimed. Meta-analysis was thus proposed as a relatively objective way of deciding which selection method or particular test has the better 'track record'.

When used to explore the relative worth of selection methods, this track-record approach is one of the reasons why psychologists tend to recommend selection methods such as work samples and measures of ability (eg general mental ability and psychomotor ability) and are very doubtful of the value of graphology. Although occasional studies have suggested that graphology may have some value, they are completely outweighed by a large number of studies which suggest that graphology has no value at all. However, in common with most statistics, results from meta-analysis can be misleading if the background to the information collected is not fully understood, for example:

- there is a general tendency for researchers and others to publish only the results that are successful; accordingly, if data used for meta-analysis is collected from the scientific literature, the picture given is likely to be biased towards what tests can do *at their best*.

- on the other hand, it would not be appropriate to use some published data in a meta-analysis. In a study between test scores and educational achievements where all possible correlations have been computed and reported, some are expected to be high and significant (eg between mechanical aptitude and engineering qualifications) while other correlations are expected to be low and insignificant (eg between mechanical aptitude and English literature). If the correlation between mechanical aptitude and English literature was included in a meta-analysis to assess the value of tests in predicting educational achievements, the results would be misleading.

Before making decisions about tests on the basis of meta-analysis it is important to know what guidelines were given to those collecting the data, the sources of the data, and whether results from particular studies were rejected for methodological or other reasons. Unfortunately such information is seldom given. Mary Tenopyr (1989) writes: 'Many meta-analyses are done on such a gross basis and reported in such brevity that the reader who does not have the opportunity to study the source data on which the meta-analysis was based may be misled'.

Validity generalisation seemed to offer an alternative approach to the apparent problems of situational specificity; mention was made earlier of the job-families approach based on statistical analyses of the Position Analysis Questionnaire and reported in 1978. For a while this approach seemed less important than meta-analysis – for example, writing in 1981, Schmidt *et al* went so far as to say the 'large task differences between jobs do not moderate the validities'. However, there was early debate about the statistics to be used, and a number of other issues have been raised subsequently. More cautious or refined views have recently been expressed; for example, Hunter and Schmidt now suggest that validity generalisation is more likely to be associated with cognitive skills.

Research into validity generalisation has continued and the ideas generated are worth consideration in practice. For example, if a particular clerical test has been a useful predictor of performance for a series of clerical jobs in an organisation, then the same test may be of worth if there are changes in the way the tasks are divided, or if new but similar tasks are introduced. However, a careful analysis of the jobs should be carried out before reaching such conclusions, and some dilemmas may arise in practice. For example:

- if a new kind of clerical work is to be introduced, are the skills which comprise the work to be done in the new situation sufficiently similar to those featuring in past studies to warrant the continued use of an existing selection test?

- if a particular test has been a useful predictor of performance for a wide range of clerical jobs, it is likely to be of some value in a new situation involving similar clerical work. However, will it be the best test, and could it be worth spending time to find a test attuned to the specific situation which may be more effective?

Work on the statistical approach to validity generalisation originated by Schmidt and Hunter continues, but so does the debate about the assumptions and methodology. All in all, the basic ideas offered by meta-analysis and validity generalisation are well worth taking into account. But remember that, however sophisticated the statistical/computer analyses, the skills used in the job for which a test is being selected should be similar (in terms of types and levels) to those on which past performance of a test or tests have been established. Indeed, a recent Industrial Tribunal decision suggests that whether or not the content of a test is directly related to the work to be done may carry more weight with the tribunal than the sophisticated statistical approaches outlined above.

John Toplis

References

COLBERT, G. A. *and* TAYLOR, L. R. (1979) 'Empirically derived job families as a foundation for the study of validity generalisation – Study 3'. *Personnel Psychology*, Vol 31, No 2, pp 355–64.

SCHMIDT, F. L. *and* HUNTER, J. E. (1977) 'Development of a general solution to the problem of validity generalization'. *Journal of Applied Psychology*, Vol 62, No 5, pp 529–40.

SCHMIDT, F. L., HUNTER, J. E. *and* PEARLMAN, K. (1981) 'Task differences as moderators of aptitude test validity in selection: A red herring'. *Journal of Applied Psychology*, Vol 66, No 2, pp 166–85.

TAYLOR, L. R. (1978) 'Empirically derived job families as a foundation for the study of validity generalisation – Study 1'. *Personnel Psychology*, Vol 3, No 2, pp 325–40.

TENOPYR, M. (1989) 'Comment on Meta-Analysis: Facts and Theories', in SMITH, M. *and* ROBERTSON, I., *Advances in Selection and Assessment.* Chichester, Wiley.

Appendix 8
The cost–benefits of improving selection

Part I Introduction

Organisations normally try to ascertain the likely benefits of taking certain courses of action, and different types of activity may also be compared. Although benefits may be of several kinds (eg direct cost or time savings, morale, reduced staff turnover), these are difficult to evaluate unless they are converted into monetary terms in some way. Thus it is possible, for instance, to estimate the savings made by reducing staff turnover by a certain percentage. Note the word 'estimate': such calculations are unlikely to be exact. However this inexactness is not unusual; all business plans are based to some extent – and often to a large extent – on estimates and forecasts.

In commercial enterprises, expression in monetary terms is necessary because their aim is to make profits (expressed financially). Other organisations, which do not share the same goal, nevertheless aim to achieve their objectives cost effectively; in order to do this all components have to be costed as accurately as possible; in some cases this is relatively easy, while in others it is extremely difficult.

In principle, the most straightforward way of evaluating the cost–benefit of a particular action or input is to ascertain its cost (eg a new machine tool), and then to measure output (eg widget production per week and/or improved quality measures). However, the latter can be obtained only after installation; if one wishes to know beforehand the likely cost–benefit of the new machine, it has to be estimated from other information, such as the experience of other organisations, the speed with which the machine processes widgets (compared with the old one), etc.

There is no fundamental difference when the new input or action is a human resources one, such as a training course or selection method, except that most managers are unaccustomed to thinking of these in financial cost–benefit terms. However, human resource changes are seldom made except in the expectation of a benefit that could ultimately be translated into monetary values.

In the light of this it has been argued that it would be useful to have methods of quantifying the cost–benefits of human resource inputs such as introducing tests in a selection procedure. The main technique that has been developed for this is known as Utility Analysis, and a great many attempts have been made to estimate cost–benefits using a number of variations on the basic procedure. As might be expected, validity figures always play a key role, preferably obtained from follow-up studies (predictive validity, see Chapter 1).

Utility analysis

Rather crude techniques for quantifying the benefits of selection procedures have existed since the 1920s, and more sophisticated ones for about 40 years, but only in the last 15 years or so has more rapid progress been made. The advances are largely due to the fact that one of the key components of the utility analysis formula, validity, can now be estimated much more accurately using meta-analysis (see Appendix 7), and much more is also now known about the most difficult aspect of the technique: estimating the value to the organisation of a good employee compared with an average or poor one (in any particular type of job).

The formula is described fully, with an example, in Part II, since the details will probably be of particular interest only to those hoping to use it. The remainder of this Part describes and discusses the components of the formula in more general terms and evaluates its own utility.

In simple terms the utility analysis formula is:

$$\text{NET BENEFIT} = \text{QUALITY} \times \text{QUANTITY} - \text{COST}$$

Quality in this context has three components:

1 the validity of the selection procedure

2 the average performance on the procedure of those selected

3 the difference, in monetary value to the employer, between an average and an above-average employee in the relevant job.

Quantity is the number of successful candidates multiplied by the average length of time (in years) that they remain employed by the organisation. Since it is in the future, this time period is unknown but can be estimated from past experience of employing similar people.

Cost is the full cost of the selection procedure, including interviewers' time, expenses, and possibly a proportion of the development costs of the procedure.

Over the years this generally-agreed basic formula has been enlarged and modified to take account of other factors, such as the cost of capital employed, inflation and tax. However, it can be argued that it is not worth complicating the formula unduly since it may never be possible to calculate the exact benefit, nor is this necessarily needed. The main concern may be the break-even point (Boudreau, 1983); if a procedure definitely has benefits that outweigh its costs it is worth using even if the organisation is uncertain of the size of the benefit. As noted earlier, decisions about selection procedures are little different in this respect from other investment decisions.

However, in practice, an organisation often has to choose between several different investments. Within the human resources area, for instance, the choice may be between a more effective selection procedure and a better training programme. The relative benefits of each of these can be estimated via utility analysis but it is unlikely to be sufficient to know the two break-even points; it may be necessary to have fairly accurate point estimates of their respective benefits. The accuracy required will depend partly on whether there is a large difference in benefit between the two procedures. A big difference is likely to show up clearly, even with rough estimates.

It is, of course, possible to do several calculations, each based on slightly different assumptions. Thus we might have a 'best' and 'worst' scenario, as well as others systematically varying the assumptions, eg selection ratio, years in employment once selected. However, most people wanting to use utility analysis in a practical situation would be best advised to keep it fairly simple.

Looking again at the basic formula,

$$\text{Net benefit} = \text{Quality} \times \text{Quantity} - \text{Cost},$$

it can easily be seen that, as would be expected, the benefit is most when costs are low and quality and/or quantity are relatively high.

The quantity component is high when:

- there are or will be a great many jobs to fill, ie if a large number of people are being selected (clearly it is more worthwhile developing a better selection procedure in such a situation)

- those selected stay in post, on average, for a reasonable length of time, ie low staff turnover (the corollary of this is that if you have developed a good selection procedure and know that it is selecting good staff, it is worth making every effort to retain these people).

The quality component of the formula is high when:

- the validity of the selection procedure is high

- employees vary greatly in worth to the organisation, ie there is a large difference between good, average and poor performance in the job. The opposite case is where there is little variability; this may occur when the job is so simple and controlled that there is little scope for individual variation. It may also occur when the variability in output is not mainly due to individuals' work performance but to factors outside their control, such as deliveries, machinery function, etc.

- the average performance of those selected is fairly high (and there are sufficient applicants to choose from).

It is important to note that one generally has limited control over most of the above components. Most recruiters, for instance, try to obtain a good pool of applicants from which to select, but this is not always possible.

It may surprise many people that the component which is most likely to be (relatively) more in the control of the recruiter is the validity of the selection procedure: it is usually possible to improve validity by, for example, training interviewers to be more effective, or introducing tests or assessment centres. There are few, if any, situations where a selection procedure is so good that it cannot be improved. However, it may be worth expending extra resources only when the job(s) are important to the organisation, and/or a fairly large number of people are likely to be recruited over the next few months or years.

Interestingly, most managers appear to appreciate the importance of validity (once they understand its meaning) to such an extent that they do not usually seem to want to calculate detailed cost–benefits when validity figures are available (as they must be, of course, since they are needed in the cost–benefit/utility analysis formula). Good evidence for this comes from research in the USA (Latham and Whyte, 1994) where over 140 managers were asked about their opinions on different kinds of information pertaining to a selection procedure: validity studies, expectancy tables, utility analysis, and a combination of all of these.

The managers had most confidence in the validity studies, and preferred to have this information alone rather than having the utility analysis which did, in any case, utilise the validity figures (and showed high returns on the investment). The reasons were not asked for, but it can be hypothesised that managers might have mistrusted such apparently exact financial figures in the personnel field. In addition, some found certain aspects of the utility analysis confusing.

Whatever their reasoning, managers were indicating their (relative) confidence in the results of validity studies; perhaps this is not too surprising because the idea behind a validity study is clear, the procedure not unduly complex and the resulting correlation is a direct measure of what we are interested in: the strength of the relationship between the test(s) (or other selection procedure) and job performance. Whilst there may be certain difficulties in evaluating job performance, it is clearly more straightforward than evaluating the difference between good and average employees in monetary terms! Similarly, interpreting correlations may not be an everyday task for many managers, but the basic idea is fairly readily grasped.

In contrast, utility analysis is much more complex, even if we take on trust the components of the formula, especially the financial value put on employees. It is possible that managers who have been personally involved in the latter procedure would be more inclined to accept the results. However, there is no research indicating this, and the precedents are not favourable: similar work in other areas has surprised researchers by showing that managers do not necessarily have greater confidence in the results of research and analyses in which they have themselves been involved.

It is also likely that managers may be wary of equating a measure of a person's job performance with that person's value to the organisation. As we shall see in the discussion of job performance in Part II, some measures of this can be very general; none the less it is unlikely that they take into account the totality of a person's potential contribution. For example, one person may be skilled at defusing awkward situations, whilst another, good at the job itself, may manage to rub everyone else up the wrong way. No unidimensional measure of job performance is likely to include these kinds of subtleties. However, it is possible to use multidimensional measures in the utility analysis formula. There is an interesting discussion of these issues in Boudreau *et al* (1994).

We may conclude that perhaps it is to be expected that managers have more faith in a fairly direct measure of the relationship between a test (or other procedure) and job performance, than in an apparently rather fancy method of calculating the financial returns from using that test. As we have seen, the validity figure can be regarded as the key component of the utility analysis formula, because the other components are relatively fixed (number to be recruited, quality of applicants, etc). If we are using utility analysis to compare different selection procedures (such as adding a test) we may as well just look at the different validities (unless we specifically need to estimate the financial returns).

In conclusion, it is worth reiterating the conditions that give rise to the greatest financial benefit, whether or not we decide to try to quantify it. Other things being equal, the cost–benefits from selection procedures are highest when one or more of the following apply:

- the validity of the selection procedure is high

- the selection ratio is low, ie there are a large number of applicants to choose from, relative to the number of vacancies

- enough applicants are of good or reasonable quality

- employees (in the relevant job) vary greatly in worth to the organisation, ie performance varies significantly.

It is also worth noting that utility analysis can be used only where there are a fair number of employees (say 30 or more) in a particular job. For example, it could be used for sales staff but probably not for sales manager (a single position).

Part II   The utility analysis formula

This section is for those who want to know about utility analysis in more detail, possibly with a view to using it themselves. We shall first look at a worked example, and then continue with a more detailed discussion of the most difficult components of the formula.

Example

Let us suppose that a company has about 70 retail outlets distributed throughout a region on locations chosen, to a large extent, for their similar retail potential. Variations in performance between outlets were originally put down mainly to unavoidable differences in location and catchment area, but it became apparent that the same outlet could also perform better (or worse) after a change of manager. Closer scrutiny revealed that there were quite large differences in performance between managers.

The organisation recruits about 20 new managers annually, and they stay in post for an average of three years. Given this turnover, there are various possibilities for improvement, all of which involve identifying the key attributes of successful store managers. The company can then, for instance, try to 'grow' its own good managers, develop appropriate training procedures and/or institute a better selection process.

Let us suppose that it decides to evaluate the cost benefit of using a more expensive and time-consuming selection procedure, an assessment centre, and compare it with the former interview-only method. (It is worth noting that assessment centres normally include interviews.)

It may be recalled from Part I that the basic utility analysis formula is:

$$\text{Net Benefit} = \text{Quality} \times \text{Quantity} - \text{Cost}$$
$$\text{ie } (r \times z \times SD) \times (N \times T) - (N \times C)$$

where

r = the validity of the selection procedure, ie the correlation between performance in the job and in the selection procedure

z = average performance on the selection procedure of those selected, expressed in the form of a standard score (z)

SD = difference in financial value to the organisation between an average and an above average employee

N = Number of candidates selected or jobs filled

T = average time (in years) that those selected are likely to remain with the organisation

C = cost per person of the selection procedure

Using the formula in our example

$$\text{QUALITY} = (r \times z \times SD)$$

r (validity) : since validity studies have not been conducted in our imaginary organisation, validity correlations obtained from meta-analyses (see Appendix 7) will be used. These are based on Smith (1988) and Hunter and Hunter (1984):

validity r for interviews = 0.19
validity r for assessment centres = 0.43

z : the z representing average performance is obtained via statistical tables using the selection ratio (the proportion of applicants selected) as a starting point.

In our example the selection ratio is 0.20, ie one in five applicants (who are seen) are accepted. Statistical tables give 0.28 as the ordinate (explained later), which has to be divided by the selection ratio:

$$0.28 \div 0.20 = 1.40$$

SD : in our example we use 40 per cent of annual salary, as salary is by far the easiest starting point for estimating the difference in performance between an average and an above-average employee in financial terms (see later discussion). In the case of shop managers, however, better measures, related to turnover and profits, are likely to be available.

If the average salary, including bonuses and benefits, is £24,000,

$$40\% \text{ of } £24,000 = £9,600$$

Bringing the three quality components together:

QUALITY $= r \times z \times SD =$
interview: $0.19 \times 1.4 \times £9,600 = £2,554$
assessment centre: $0.43 \times 1.4 \times £9,600 = £5,779$

Bringing the two quantity components together:

QUANTITY $= N \times T$ where N = 20 (candidates selected per year)
and T = 3 (average number of years in post)
$N \times T = 20 \times 3 = 60$

The last component of the formula is cost:
COST means the full cost of each of the selection procedures, ie interview and assessment centre.

To ease calculations the average cost of interviewing one candidate will be taken as £150. This allows for two interviewers, clerical time and candidate's expenses. The cost of the assessment centre will be taken as £1,000 per candidate. This includes planning and running the procedure, accommodation, assessors' time, candidate's expenses, and a proportion of the cost of producing or buying in the procedure.

Multiplying these per person costs by the number of candidates (100 per year) gives:

Total annual cost of:

interviewing: $100 \times £150 = £15,000$
assessment centres: $100 \times £1,000 = £100,000$

Lastly, bringing together all three elements of the formula:
Monetary benefit of selecting 20 store managers a year:

Net Benefit = Quality × Quantity – Cost

Interview: $(£2,554 \times 60) - £15,000 = £138,240$
Assessment centre: $(£5,779 \times 60) - £100,000 = £246,740$

Net benefit of assessment centres over using interviews only:

$£246,740 - £138,240 = £108,500$

Further discussion
As illustrated in the above example, it is the quality components of the utility analysis formula that present us with the most problems. As quantity and cost are relatively straightforward, we will focus here on the three components of Quality: r, z, and SD.

i) r : the validity (accuracy) of the selection procedure. This is expressed in the form of a correlation (r) between performance in the selection procedure and a measure of job performance. It is not necessarily essential to calculate r afresh for each situation since much is already known about the validity of different selection methods, especially via meta-analysis (see Appendix 7).

ii) z : average performance in the selection procedure expressed in the form of a standard score (z), in order to achieve comparability between different selection methods. Standard scores are a type of standard deviation (a measure of variability, like 'range of scores' but much more sophisticated). They are derived from the normal distribution curve (see Figure 3). It is not necessary to understand the theory behind this, since there are statistical tables giving the area and height (ordinate) at different points on the normal curve. We first need to find the ordinate for our particular selection ratio (proportion of applicants accepted).

For instance, if one in three applicants are accepted the selection ratio is 0.33. (This is the area of the smaller section of the normal curve, the larger area representing the unselected candidates.) Looking up the ordinate for a ratio of 0.33 gives us 0.36. We then divide the selection ratio by this figure, ie 0.36 ÷ 0.33 = 1.09, which represents the standard score of those selected if the selection procedure is perfect and always selects the top third.

In practice the procedure is not perfect, as the validity correlation indicates; a perfect procedure would give a correlation of +1, whilst random selection would give 0. To obtain an estimate of the actual standard score of those selected, the 'perfect' z must be multiplied by the validity (r), as happens in the utility analysis formula. Thus, if the validity is 0.4 and the 'perfect' standard score is 1.09, as above, the adjusted standard score is $z = 0.4 \times 1.09 = 0.44$. This figure is, in effect, an estimate of the improvement over random selection obtained by using a selection procedure with a validity of 0.4, where a third of the applicants are accepted for employment. Since we are concerned with the monetary value of selection, we need to translate this into financial terms. This is achieved via the last component of the *quality* part of the equation, SD.

iii) SD : difference in financial value to the organisation between an average employee and an above-average one. This is the most difficult part of the utility analysis formula. However, the first part of the argument is generally accepted: how an average and an above-average employee should be defined.

It is reasonable to suppose that, like most things, work performance is normally distributed, ie most people are near the average and there are fewer and fewer people as one moves towards the two extremes of very poor and very good (see Figure 3). If this is the case, one standard deviation (SD) above the average (mean) is, by definition, a performance attained only by the top 15 per cent of workers; this is the point at which 15 per cent perform better and 85 per cent worse (see Figure 3). If the monetary value to the employer of a worker at this point can be assessed, and also the value of an average worker, the difference between these two is the figure required by the formula (SD).

However, expressing the difference between a good and an average employee in financial terms is not usually a straightforward matter, although managers and supervisors have managed to do this for many jobs. Several different approaches have been tried with different sorts of work; for instance, the view can be taken that an employee is worth what the employer is willing to pay for that person's services. Research (Schmidt and Hunter, 1983) indicates that the standard deviation (SD) may be roughly 40 per cent of salary, and it may well be more than this (40–70 per cent has been suggested).

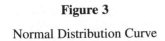

Figure 3

Normal Distribution Curve

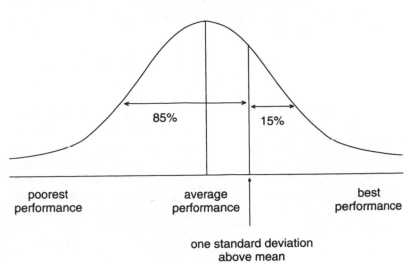

Attempts have also been made to calculate the standard deviation by cost accounting methods, but these have proved laborious and often of dubious accuracy. More recently a combination of cost accounting and managers' estimates has been proposed (Judiesch *et al*, 1992). This seems promising as it uses each method for what it is best suited to, and not for the aspect where it has proved weaker (see discussion in Cook, 1993). Cost accounting can produce an average financial return figure much more easily than it can estimate the difference in value between good and bad workers. Conversely, managers and supervisors usually have a fairly good idea of the differences between good, average and poor workers, but do not know what an average worker is really worth to the organisation (unless salary is used). Minor differences in the wording of instructions to managers have also been shown to affect their estimates significantly.

The proposed solution is to use cost accounting to find the value of the average employee (in the relevant job) and then, with this starting point, managers and supervisors can much more easily and reliably produce estimates of the difference between an average and an above-average employee in financial terms. In practice many managers may meet to agree this, or the average of their different estimates may be taken.

This method seems likely to produce a more accurate assessment of the SD component of the formula, but total accuracy is unlikely to be achieved for most jobs. It may be safer to err on the conservative side and underestimate the value of employees. However there is also a danger in gross underestimation.

As mentioned in Part I, to obtain a more accurate estimate of financial benefit it is best to incorporate other elements of cost accounting into the basic formula. These include allowing for inflation, tax and the cost of capital employed. A lower, more conservative, estimate is then obtained so it is worth noting that these same elements should be incorporated when evaluating any other investment. It is also possible to underestimate the potential benefits of having better staff, such as their effect on other staff and the fact that they may be promoted and accrue further benefits to the organisation. Also, the formula looks only at one intake, or one year's intake, whereas, in practice, recruitment is an ongoing process. Readers wanting to pursue this subject further may wish to consult Boudreau (1983).

References

BOUDREAU, J. W. (1983) 'Economic considerations in estimating the utility of human resource productivity improvement programs'. *Personnel Psychology*, 36. pp551–576.

BOUDREAU, J. W., STURMAN, M. C. *and* JUDGE, T. A. (1994) 'Utility analysis: what are the black boxes, and do they affect decisions?' In ANDERSON, N. *and* HERRIOT, P. (eds), *Assessment and Selection in Organisations: Methods and Practice in Recruitment and Appraisal. First Update and Supplement 1994.* pp77–96. Chichester, Wiley.

COOK, M. (1993) *Personnel Selection and Productivity*, 2nd ed. Chichester, Wiley.

HUNTER, J. E. *and* HUNTER, R. (1984) 'Validity and utility of alternative predictors of job performance'. *Journal of Applied Psychology*, 68. pp407.

JUDIESCH, M. K., SCHMIDT, F. L. *and* MOUNT, M. K. (1992) 'Estimates of the dollar value of employee output in utility analysis: an empirical test of two theories'. *Journal of Applied Psychology*, 77. pp234–250.

Latham, G. P. *and* Whyte, G. (1994) 'The futility of utility analysis'. *Personnel Psychology*, 47. pp31–46.

Schmidt, F. L. *and* Hunter, J. E. (1983) 'Individual differences in productivity: an empirical test of estimates derived from studies of selection procedure utility'. *Journal of Applied Psychology*, 96. pp72–98.

Schmidt, F. L., Hunter, J. E., McKenzie, R. C. *and* Muldrow, T. W. (1979) 'Impact of valid selection procedures on workforce productivity'. *Journal of Applied Psychology*, 64. pp609–626.

Smith, M. (1988) 'Calculating the sterling value of selection'. *Guidance and Assessment Review*, Vol.4, No.1. pp6–8.

Smith, M., Gregg, M. *and* Andrews, D. (1989). *Selection and Assessment: A new appraisal.* Chapter 9. London, Pitman.

The first exposition of the complete underlying rationale of modern utility analysis is given in a technical paper by Schmidt, Hunter, McKenzie and Muldrow (1979, see above), together with an example using computer programmers. Alternative simpler expositions and examples of use for non-technical readers are given in the two Smith references. There is a further useful discussion in the book by Cook.

The relevant journals (mainly the *Journal of Applied Psychology*, but sometimes *Personnel Psychology*, both US-based publications) also contain many examples of utility analysis in use, and discussions of methodological issues.

Most good statistics books (you do not need on advanced text) give statistical tables relating to the normal curve that can be used for looking up ordinates. The tables used here appear in:

Guilford, J. P. *and* Fruchter, B. (1978) *Fundamental statistics in Psychology and Education*, 6th ed. Tokyo, McGraw-Hill Kogakusha.

Appendix 9
Taking tests and receiving feedback

As a whole, this book has been written for managers. However, managers are sometimes asked about testing by colleagues, relatives or friends who may have little or no experience of testing and who may wonder if they can prepare for the experience in any way. This appendix has been written with such enquiries in mind.

The first part of this appendix deals with taking tests as part of a selection procedure; the second part deals briefly with obtaining 'feedback' from employers, while the remainder deals with taking tests as part of counselling or guidance.

From the start it is important to be clear which kind of situation you are going to be facing, since terms such as 'development centre' can cause confusion – sometimes development centres are an opportunity to discuss your future with independent facilitators who are there to help you, and none of the information that you give the assessors will be passed on to your employer or to any other third party; however, other 'development centres' may in fact be part of a selection process and you must then expect all the information that you reveal to be used in the decision-making process.

At the start of a well-designed selection process, you should be given clear information about the vacancy and about the kind of person that the employer is seeking to fill it. This will help you decide whether or not you should apply. Written applications (on applications forms or with curricula vitae) are normally requested so that the most promising applicants can be selected on the basis of the applications and invited to attend the selection procedure. If you are invited to a well-designed selection procedure you should be sent a number of details in advance including (a) where the procedure is taking place (b) when you should arrive (c) who will be there to meet you (d) the people who will assess you (e) the selection techniques that will be used (eg the types of tests, the other procedures that will be involved etc) (f) when a decision will be made (g) whether you will be reimbursed for travelling or other expenses.

The notes that follow deal only with preparation for testing.

Taking tests as part of a selection procedure

To be successful at a selection procedure you must reach the required standard. If there are more applicants than vacancies (and this is nearly always the case) you must also show that you are one of the better candidates. Often there is only one vacancy and, if that is the case, you will have to show that you are the best candidate overall.

If the selection procedure involves reasoning or similar tests you may be given a test description handout in advance of the procedure. The handout may tell you how the test will be presented to you (eg paper-and-pencil or computer-based), how long it will last, and how you will be expected to make your replies (eg writing the answer, or shading boxes on a form for computer scoring). Most importantly, the handout may give examples of the kinds of question that you may be facing in the test itself.

If you have little or no experience of the test items shown as examples, you may wish to practice by referring to books which contain similar questions (and which provide answers too); these might be school or college text books dealing with a specific subject, eg how to calculate percentages, or it may be worth looking at books on psychology which contain examples of questions used in reasoning tests. In deciding whether or not to prepare, consider the following points:

- Is there any information about whether the example items are representative of the rest of the test, or whether they merely illustrate some of the items in the test? For example, does a sample question involving percentages mean that all the questions involve percentages, or does it mean that there is a variety of mathematical calculations in the test itself, including percentages, fractions, decimals etc? Although the test should reflect the content of the work to be done if you are successful, it might be prudent to check this point with the person arranging the selection procedure.

- If the test items reflect abilities or skills that you have not used recently, and if there is time to practise, it may be worth investing some time and effort in researching and practising the skills. On the other hand, if the test items reflect abilities and skills that you have always found difficult, you may decide to withdraw on this occasion; if you really want to pass the test and to be offered that kind of work, it might be better to prepare over a period of time, perhaps even enrolling for relevant courses at a local college or elsewhere.

213

If the selection procedure involves personality questionnaires or similar techniques, it will not be appropriate to revise by going to the library and looking in books. The aim of such questionnaires is to build up a pattern of your interests and preferences, your likes and dislikes. Accordingly, your preparation might be in terms of:

- reflecting on the things that you prefer to do, that you enjoy, etc and contrasting these with situations that you prefer to avoid, dislike etc

- reflecting on your personal flexibility; think about the extent to which you are willing to do work that does not interest you in order to take on a new job and to be successful at it

- reflecting on the extent to which your preferences and other behaviours really affect you; for example, most people are a little apprehensive before making a presentation – think about whether you are someone who is really nervous or just a little apprehensive

- finally, looking at the results of any previous assessments, think about whether you felt (and whether others felt) that the profile was a fair reflection of how you feel, and about the way that you are likely to come across to others; might this influence how you answer the questions this time?

Personality questionnaires do not have right or wrong answers. What happens is that a number of questions are designed to measure a particular quality (eg self-confidence); a person who indicates high self-confidence on each of the individual questions will have a profile that indicates a high level of self-confidence overall.

There is a fine line between answering the questions in a way that is likely to give a 'true' picture of your personality, preferences etc, and answering the questions in a way that may increase your chances of getting a job. For example, someone lacking in self-confidence might be tempted to describe themselves as being confident in order to get a job. However, few employers rely solely on replies to personality questionnaires so the deception may be found with ease; further, if the deception were to work, there is the issue of whether a timid applicant could cope with the job demanding self-confidence in practice.

Obtaining 'feedback' from employers

Whether or not you are successful, it is worth asking for 'feedback' about your performance not only on the tests but in other ways. It will be helpful if you can clarify whether you met the standard for the job – if you did it might be worth applying again in the future or seeking a similar job elsewhere. If you did not, it might be worth reflecting on whether you might be seen as a stronger applicant for a different kind of work (see below).

So far as your performance on the reasoning tests is concerned, try to clarify:

- whether you reached the required standard overall
- whether any errors you may have made were in response to a particular kind of question, eg did you get all the percentages wrong?

So far as your replies to personality and similar questionnaires are concerned, try to establish:

- whether your profile was in line with the kind of profile generally sought for this kind of work
- whether a particular kind of profile was being sought in order to 'fit' with the rest of the team, and whether, and in what ways, your profile matched it.

In the light of this feedback you will need to decide:

- whether your responses to the questionnaire gave a fair picture of yourself
- whether you feel that the implications drawn from your profile were fair to you.

This may influence the way that you reply to future questionnaires or the way that you discuss the resulting profiles with potential employers.

Commercial pressures mean that few employers feel that they can afford to give detailed feedback to unsuccessful candidates, and some may fear debating outcomes in case it is the first sign of the decision being taken to an industrial tribunal. Even though you may have spent a day or more attending the selection procedure, employers tend to lose interest in unsuccessful applicants once selection decisions have been made. Accordingly, the way that you ask for feedback may be critical in terms of the response that you get; a telephone enquiry seeking information in a few areas may be more successful than a formal request seeking detailed written feedback.

Taking tests as part of counselling or guidance

If your only experience of taking tests is as part of a selection procedure for a job, you may not experience the full benefit of testing. There are several reasons:

- The tests that you are asked to take are likely to be closely related to the specific vacancy; accordingly, even if the employer is willing to give you feedback it can be only in relation to the particular vacancy; there may be little indication of which kind of work you might do best or which kind of work would best suit you.

- Few employers can offer a very wide range of jobs or have staff with the skills to offer career advice.

For this reason, people sometimes seek professional advice to check that they have identified the strongest of their abilities and to ensure that they have a good understanding of their motivation and preferences and of the way that they come across to others. Advice can help target their job applications or construct personal development plans with a view to developing strengths and overcoming any shortcomings. Sometimes important dilemmas need to be identified and resolved; for example, some people are bored by what they can do and set their minds on jobs for which they have little or no experience; they then become frustrated by the predictable rejections.

Other parts of this book have drawn attention to the dangers of seeking advice about testing from people who have little or no training and no recognised qualifications. Excellent free advice can sometimes be obtained from chartered psychologists and others working for careers services, university appointments services etc.

John Toplis

Appendix 10
An example of an external assessment report

This example (the candidate details given are, of course, fictitious) is based on an assessment procedure where the candidate had been referred for external assessment by a major investment bank.

The report is based primarily on psychometric tests, including two personality measures and four cognitive ability tests. The procedure also included an interview of about two hours. All test scores are quoted in relation to specific senior management norms. This is, of course, but one example of how such reports can be presented and structured; there are many variations, some of which suit particular needs better than others.

**PERSONAL
IN CONFIDENCE**

EXTERNAL ASSESSMENT REPORT

Name A B Jones

Date 24 July 1991

Assessor Dr Clive Fletcher

This report is primarily concerned with judgements about how the candidate will behave at work; the consultant has formed these views from the individual's CV, from interpretation of the psychometrics, and from discussion with the candidate in an in-depth interview.

The report is less concerned with the reasons why the individual will behave in any particular way; nor does it comment on technical or professional competence.

The information given here must be treated as strictly confidential and should be made available only to staff who have responsibility for employment or career planning decisions relating to this individual. The report should not be used if more than three years have elapsed since it was written.

Name Alan Border Jones

Date of Birth 20 April 1957

Age 34

EDUCATIONAL/PROFESSIONAL QUALIFICATIONS

1970–75 Astonbury College

A levels in Maths, Economics, English, General Studies

S level English

1975–78 & 1981–82 Bristol University

BSc Joint Hons (2:1) Economics and Accountancy

MSc Quantitative Analysis

CAREER HISTORY

1978–80 Jones Bros   Articled Clerk

1981–91 XYZ Co   Assistant finance manager (1985)

                  Economic analyst (1986)

                  Head of division (1989)

219

Intellectual effectiveness

Synopsis
Mr Jones has a good level of intellectual effectiveness. Compared to senior managers as a group, he is average on numerical (but see comments below on this) and imaginative thinking abilities, above average on verbal ability and outstanding in logical thinking ability. He had not taken any psychometric tests before, and was somewhat sceptical in his attitude to them. Also, he was both a little tired and distracted by his activities immediately prior to attending the session.

Numerical ability
His score on the test of his ability to make correct decisions and inferences from numerical and statistical data was average. However, he had asked whether in the marking of the test there was any penalty for errors. He was told that there was not, but that an accuracy score would be computed. This perhaps affected his strategy, as he worked rather slowly but with 100% accuracy. His score may reflect his cautious strategy, and may underestimate his true ability.

Verbal ability
He scored at the upper end of the average range, in the top 20 per cent of senior managers, on the test of vocabulary and verbal reasoning. In conversation, he expresses himself clearly and well. His spelling is a trifle erratic, though.

Logical thinking
His performance on the test of critical thinking, covering the dispassionate analysis of information, arguments, inferences and deductions, was outstanding and places him in the top 15 per cent of senior managers. He took longer than most to complete the test, but he has excellent analytical ability.

Imaginative thinking
The test of the quantity and quality of his ideas showed him to be just about average in both respects. He was somewhat uneven in his performance, and does not seem to be all that imaginative.

Work approach

General approach
Mr Jones is above all a thoughtful individual who approaches things in a rather intellectual and dispassionate manner. He likes to ask questions, to probe beneath the surface and to feel that he has a sound grasp of the issues before he commits himself. He will work in a thoroughly prepared and highly structured way.

Productivity
He has a good level of drive and will tackle his objectives with speed and vigour. He may not be all that swift in getting action off the ground in the first place, but when he does move forward, it will be in an efficient and organised way. His productivity will be above average.

Quality of work
He will place considerable emphasis on quality, and will expect high standards of himself and of others. He is deeply thoughtful and will plan ahead, showing excellent awareness of the strategic picture. There may be occasions when he over-analyses issues, and over-complicates them as a result. Also, he will fare better when dealing with problems that call for convergent rather than divergent thinking; he is not (outside his specialism) an ideas man. But for the most part, he will think things through carefully and produce high quality work.

Mastery of detail
He will be careful and attentive to detail, and will seek to minimise errors. He will perhaps spend a little too long on details, if anything.

Decision-making
He will be fairly cautious in his approach to decisions, and will prefer to take some time to think them through and to cover all the issues. He will take only well-calculated risks. When he has made up his mind, he will be difficult to sway. His analytical ability is excellent, and his judgement will prove to be sound.

Tolerance of pressure
Mr Jones is emotionally stable and resilient. He does perhaps have more feelings than might be apparent from his way of presenting himself, but he is controlled in the way he expresses them. He has more than enough resources of intellect and energy to cope with pressure. He has in the

recent past had to tolerate very considerable domestic and work pressures.

Flexibility
He is not perhaps the most flexible of people. He likes to operate in a highly structured manner, and to work from the basis of careful analysis and planning. He will feel less comfortable having to react quickly in conditions of ambiguity and uncertainty. Also, there will be times when he is a trifle rigid in his attitude to others.

Ambition
He is quite ambitious, though he claims to have no desire to be an MD. He will be driven mainly by intellectual challenge and by the need to prove himself to others.

Relationships with others

General impact
Mr Jones has a broadly positive attitude to other people. He is very sociable and gregarious, but he likes to be in control of his interactions with others, which may at times cause some problems. He will make a favourable impression on first meeting, if he wants to do so.

Relationships with superiors
Superiors will find that he is keen to take responsibility and to exercise greater authority, though he will not usually take this to the extent that is causes problems. He will want a boss who takes a strategic perspective and who will be ready to spend time discussing issues with him in some depth. Those above him will find that he listens but makes up his own mind; he will be independent and confident in his views, and will certainly not accept something simply because his boss thinks it is correct. He will put over his ideas with conviction and will argue his case in a determined fashion. His manner will sometimes be more direct than diplomatic, and he will need a boss who is both intellectually confident and not too sensitive or easily offended. Superiors will find that he can take criticism and that he is willing to learn.

Relationships with peers
Peers will find him to be outgoing and fairly friendly; he will enjoy mixing with them socially. They will appreciate his open mindedness

and his willingness to evaluate ideas on their merits. However, they will also find that he likes to be in control; he will take the leadership role whenever possible and will want to guide the decision-making process in the direction he feels (after consulting others) is best. He will enjoy debating issues and will communicate his thinking to his peers in a confident manner – he will be influential and persuasive. They will find that he is occasionally rather tactless; he perhaps does not realise that other people lack his detachment and resilience. For the most part, he will co-operate effectively as part of a team and will display a reasonable amount of patience with those around him.

Relationships with subordinates
He will organise the work of those under him in a thorough and efficient manner, laying down a rigid framework for them to operate within. He will delegate reasonably willingly, but he will tend to monitor his subordinates' work quite closely and may slightly inhibit their scope for initiative. He will, however, be very willing to listen and to take on board ideas – though he will expect his subordinates to have thought things through carefully first, and he will analyse and debate their proposals for action very fully. Staff will probably find that he is not all that sensitive to their emotional needs or personal circumstances; he can appreciate their feelings and problems in an intellectual way when his attention is drawn to them, but without showing much empathy. He will set demanding targets and will drive those under him to achieve high standards. He will manage high quality, intellectually able and self-motivated staff well enough (though some may find him to be a little too controlling). His handling of more junior staff, or of individuals who are more temperamental may not be so adept, however.

Summary and integration

Mr Jones is a man who places considerable emphasis on a detached, dispassionate and intellectual approach to problems and issues. He is a deeply thoughtful man who likes to evaluate ideas and to debate them; he will not be willing to take things at face value and will always seek to question and to delve deeper before making up his mind. In general, this will prove to be most effective in helping him to attain high standards. He will plan and organise his activities with considerable thoroughness. He is outstanding in his capacity for logical analysis, and has a good level of intellectual effectiveness overall. There may be occasions, though, when he indulges in a little too much analysis, and where his caution and need to understand in full reduces his flexibility and speed of response.

There is also some danger that he overly-intellectual in his response to others. He is highly objective and rather emotionally detached, and he is not all that strong in his ability to empathise. He perhaps finds it a little harder than most really to appreciate and understand how other people feel. Consequently, he may be a trifle insensitive and tactless at times. He is quite thick-skinned himself and probably does not realise that his direct and logical approach can be conveyed in a manner that is not always well received. This is to some extent exacerbated by his assertive nature; he likes to take the lead and to be the centre of attention, and he will be quite a dominating presence at times. He is well able to understand others on a purely intellectual level, and can deal with their problems and reactions in this way. But where he is faced with individuals who are more temperamental and less well emotionally controlled than he is, he will struggle.

Mr Jones has a high level of drive and will be energetic and vigorous in the way he pursues his objectives. He is a confident and socially outgoing man who will make an impact on those around him, usually wielding influence and being persuasive. He will listen to other people's ideas, then make up his mind – and once he has made it up, he will not be easy to shift. He is not someone who is willing to fall into line very readily. He will want to be in a position to determine the decisions taken. He structures the work of those under him in a thorough and efficient way, exerting close control and setting demanding targets.

Evaluation of A B Jones for the post of director of economic research, Anybank Corp

Main assets

- Good intellectual level; outstanding in logical analysis
- Ample drive; will attain above average productivity
- Thinks things through thoroughly and plans ahead; impressive level of strategic awareness
- Careful, structured approach to work
- Emotionally stable and resilient; able to tolerate pressure
- Judgement likely to be sound and well-considered